Foreword

I want to take you on a journey. Mine may have started innocently enough, but when it did, I started a process that became the most excruciating and rewarding thing I ever allowed myself to go through.

It started one day with a phone call. Something my son Billy did made me feel embarrassed and I heaped my own shame and desire to conceal my shame upon him.

The perfect little picture I had painted of my life seemed to be crumbling when he told me what he did. In hindsight, you might wonder why I was so embarrassed if I told you what it was, but for some reason it just tore right into my soul.

You see, I wanted everyone to believe that I did well for myself and had it all together. I wanted people to see that I was a successful business owner and that I raised my kids right. Everything they did was overseen by my judgments. After all, your kids are a reflection of you, right? I did not want them to reflect poorly on the image I was projecting of myself.

After a heated conversation over the phone about this embarrassment, I ordered my son to keep this to himself and not to tell anyone. I didn't actually counsel him or console him. I just instinctively commanded him to NOT tell a soul!

He seemed to be growing more agitated over the phone. He said back to me in a sterile, stern voice, "Mom, this is not about you, I don't live in your perfect little world. This happened. If I want to shout it from the roof, it's my right. It's my life. I made a mistake and if I am afraid of what people think or know that I did then I'm not being honest about who I am. I made a mistake. I paid for it and I'm not going to pretend it didn't happen."

This made me feel like my whole world was falling apart. I felt like my entire life was just make believe, a pure fantasy I had elaborately created to erase my past.

This was the beginning of the unravelling.

I cried. I realized that I had so much pent up pain. I realized I had projected my desire for people to accept me based on my success as a parent. I had made my children a measure of my accomplishment. For this reason, it became important for me that my children appear perfect.

But as I thought about this phone call, I realized this was not about my kids. I mean, the issue wasn't about them. Sure, their life and decisions were about them, but me being tied up in knots because they were being real was all on me.

I had pent up feelings of unworthiness. I had a powerful hunger to be told I was good enough, that I was special.

When you are abused as a helpless child, you are often told to be quiet. You are told not to tell and not to share about your pain or the reality of your home life.

If you talk, you are not going to be loved. Nobody will believe you. Your own parents may threaten to disown you.

My answer now when my children come to me with some confession or problem is, "Whatever you do, I will still love you and respect you."

If my children hid in the dark, as I did, that was understandable. They hid in the dark from me, until I made it safe for them to come out.

Because I became free, because I broke those cycles, I can welcome and accept my children unconditionally. I can also love and accept myself unconditionally. I want to reach back to grab a hold of others' hands and pull them out of the darkness of their fears.

If this book triggers you, sit down, and sit with it for a while. Ask yourself, "why am I triggered, what do I have to believe to feel this way, what are my beliefs about this?"

A strong word of caution: this book is meant to help you. Please do not judge any of the characters in this book. All the perceptions of things are my own. If you get lost in the trees judging people in this book, you have missed the point entirely.

I wrote this book for you. But I started writing it for me. It was my journey. My struggles and battles with my own awareness, with real things that came rudely crashing into my own perfect self-image which I wore like a cloak to cover the real me.

I went from denying and hiding the things that made me feel rejection and shame, to sharing them widely and without reservation. I don't do so out of any bad feelings or anger toward anyone.

The people and places here form a backdrop to this journey I'm taking you on with me. Keep your eyes on this inner journey and it will change you. Keep your eyes on the people and places and you will miss your gift.

Do you want to keep going along the path you are on?

I'm proof that YOU can change the direction of your life. Yes, you have to get real and sit in your funk and not spare yourself. But there you will find mercy and grace and truth, and there you will start a process, slower at first, of actually building your own life, your own identity, your own true self.

While, yes, I started writing for me, I finished for you. It wasn't easy and, at times, I wanted to run from it because I realized I was not alone. So many other people have deeply felt shame and judgment they carry inside like some sort of poison. That poison, kept down most of the time through your façade, comes out and burns people around you.

Join me on my journey, and you may take your own inner journey, away from the grip of your own inner condemnation and toward self-actualization.

Chapter 1

I finally called Mom after two years of not talking. As I entered her number and heard the dial tone blare in my ear, my heart clenched. I kept tapping the floor with my foot. I flashed to a memory of myself at six years old, when my older sister Thelma and I ran around the living room arguing over a toy. My mom, sitting in her chair, was seemingly annoyed and anxious from looking at us. She said we were making her sick. "I can't breathe," she added, grabbing a brown paper bag and beginning to inhale and exhale. I started to see her sick whenever I was around her, even without Thelma. Although this hurt me, I became numb to her always seeming to be ill around me. I accepted I'd never understand Mom.

Mom didn't pick up, which felt like a relief. I texted her instead. I dreaded this conversation since I hadn't spoken to her or any family members except my sister and brothers. After being ripped away from those I loved again and again, I had no feelings—no emotions left, especially for Mom. Her words annoyed me as we exchanged pleasantries via text. That first "Hello" back from her made my already shaky palms shakier. I girded myself for the lies I was sure she'd tell me again. She rejected me all of her life. All I could do was reject her back.

My reason for calling wasn't voluntary, but I had an assignment: my husband, Jose, and I were preparing for a two-week retreat in Panama centered around ancestral healing. The first part of our pre-trip homework— three months before getting on the plane to Panama—was to explore our heritage with questions and then finally get a true, ethnic understanding of our ancestry through a DNA test. Before the call with Mom, I'd talked with my 51-year-old brother Billy, who, along with his twin, Paul, was eleven months younger than me. He'd already taken a DNA test, and that seemed like enough information for me to use as a conversation starter with Mom.

After the initial jitters, I began grilling Mom about our heritage: what kind of food did my ancestors eat? Where exactly did they come from? These weren't easy questions for me to ask, since I never enjoyed dwelling on my family, but I kept reminding myself of my purpose. I was determined to heal from relationships in the past. The more questions I asked Mom, the more defensive she got, her answers becoming shorter and curter.

"Why are you digging up the past?" she asked via text. Clearly, we still didn't have a good relationship. She was being her normal defensive self around me. After our text exchange, I felt like I had more questions than answers. I called Thelma.

"Angel, there are so many family secrets," explained Thelma. She sighed deeply. I could feel her shaking her head on the other end of the phone. Although Mom had put her eldest daughter in charge of making legal and personal decisions for her, Thelma still seemed to struggle with Mom's near non-existent communication skills. "It's like talking to a brick wall," she admitted.

Frustrated, I ended the call with more questions than answers. It was the exact opposite of the goal Jose and I had when we first booked this trip: to heal from our pasts. This was something we loved doing together, one of our many healing adventures. After seeing how my past relationships—whether with family or previous partners—were often abusive or reactive, I was open to the concept of ancestral healing. I wanted to heal for my children, too, and show them what it could look like to find healing. After my guarded conversations with Mom, though, I wasn't sure how much further I wanted to go with this ancestral assignment.

The two other pre-trip assignments seemed easier to do: change my diet to be healthier so I could partake in the traditional ayahuasca ceremonies, and read the book, *The Disobedience of the Daughter of the Sun*, to see how patterns are passed down in families. Perhaps my mom wouldn't, or *couldn't*, answer my questions, but I could at least get this reading assignment done before we set off on our grand and, hopefully, healing adventure.

Hidden at the southern tip of San Cristobal Island was a remote tropical paradise retreat called Coco Vivo, located on 145 acres of jungle in Bocas Del Toro, Panama. As we boated to the retreat, I took in the beautiful, luminous water and playful dolphins. You could take a boat into the middle of the ocean, jump in, and watch the ocean glow. We stayed in a screened-in hut without electricity. To access the retreat meeting space every day, we had to walk up a hill. Monkeys and sloths eyed us as we walked through their living spaces.

Jose and I fell into a morning routine of taking a cold shower outside of our hut, which overlooked the translucent water. We made the best of our little outside toilet that went straight into the water. If we had to do more than pee, we used one of the outhouses and risked cockroaches scuttling under our feet. Regular toilets were only in the retreat area. This is where we'd meet the other retreat attendees for discussion, ceremony, and healthy meals, where we would drink ayahuasca and see what insights it gave us.

After I took my shower and dressed, I walked to the retreat area with Jose. He and I saw the other attendees sitting in a circle on the floor. The retreat area was a spacious, open room dappled in sunshine that overlooked the ocean. Red and green macaws and blue parrots chirped in the trees, reminding me I was in the thick of the jungles in Panama. The people who ran the retreat might as well have been Adam and Eve, presiding over the group.

A short Peruvian shaman named Lorena, and Brian, her tall, lanky boyfriend, looked over the group as Jose and I found our spots in the circle. From the serene look on her face, Lorena clearly had a deep sense of where she was from. She began talking about how her family background helped her connect to her spirit guides and her true self.

"It's important to understand your heritage," she said, "because it's carried through your DNA. The actions of your parents and grandparents back then affect you in your own life."

Lorena also talked in depth about her background, including her mom. Lorena was raised like I was, in a home that was often difficult. She had to find her own way. At least she knew her relatives, and respected and forgave them. I nodded, but the more I listened to her being so open and forgiving, the more I recoiled. I didn't respect or forgive most of my family. I couldn't possibly see myself in the same headspace as Lorena, letting go of relatives' words and deeds as successfully as she did. Although I was here to heal in the company of other people, hearing about the cycles affecting generations of family members in this space without the boundary of a book or a phone was beginning to bring me to a boil.

Despite the gleaming water, fresh food, and chirping birds and how much I wanted to find this ancestral healing along with Jose, I began to regret my decision. My conversations with Mom had been so unsatisfying. Her responses were so cold and aloof.

Why are you digging up the past?

One-by-one, the circle of people began sharing stories of their traumas and adversities. Tuning them out, I told myself *things happen to people. Horrible things happen to good people. End of story.* Talking anymore about it, like everyone else was, was simply creating negative energy. I wanted none of it.

I struggled to keep my hot tears and temper from bubbling to the surface. There was nothing transformative or pleasant I could tell the group. It was as if the devil was coming out of me.

"Not everybody understands where they come from," I finally blurted out, my arms crossed over my chest. "I'm my own person."

"It's important to discover your heritage," Lorena said. She became more irritatingly calm as my anger grew. "That's why the DNA test is important, to understand your bloodline."

"None of this matters to me anymore," I said, my voice pinched and short.

"I hear you being defensive, Angel," she said.

I started to cry. Everyone else was embracing their ancestral journey except me. I had lost my reason for exploring my heritage the longer I sat in the group. Listening to people facing their traumas made me want to run away and forget about the entire experience. Perhaps I only thought I was ready for this healing. Now, I itched to pack my bag and fly home.

The next morning, I didn't want to go back to the circle. Resisting the process of discovering my ancestry and childhood seemed to be shutting down parts of me. I still hadn't taken the DNA test. Although I didn't expect a surprising result, the anticipation of understanding my exact DNA background seemed worse than the news itself. At least that's what my body felt. What would happen if I truly understood where I came from?

Jose didn't understand why I was withdrawing from the group. I pushed him away and isolated myself in our hut, feeling like I would jump out of my skin. I began counting the days until we flew home, although we were only halfway through the retreat. Only an angelic girl named Faith managed to coax me out of my hut. I still felt as if everyone was looking at me, but she waited for me to come up. "Everyone loves you," she said.

"I know," I said, "I just feel like I can't do it." She had such a gentle spirit and seemed so kind, and made me feel so safe. I decided to go with her. When Faith convinced me to return to the circle, Lorena separated Jose and me in the group. I had to sit by myself in that big, flat room. I felt as though he supported the group thinking I had been too defensive yesterday. I felt so alone, as if I had nobody at all. I wanted to scream and get out of there.

"What's going on with you, Angel?" asked Lorena, seeing the deepening lines of anger on my face. I started crying for the second day in a row. I wanted to get back to my life, back to my success, and far, far away from what had become an interrogation into my past life.

Toward the end of the trip, I stopped talking to people altogether. I would only speak when I needed food passed to me. Although Jose wanted to hang out with everyone, he saw I needed more of him, even as I didn't want him—or anyone—to touch me. When we took a boat back to the mainland of Panama City, Panama, Jose and I ventured out on our own, away from the group for the first time in two weeks. He grabbed my hand, showing he was there for me. We were back to being physically connected since we had left the circle, back to knowing we had each other, ancestors or not. Then, Jose gave me a confident, encouraging smile. A million conversations happened with just one look.

Two weeks after our trip, the DNA tests arrived. I opened the box on my kitchen table to reveal a small glass vial. The instructions said to spit into the vial until it was full, shake it thoroughly, then send it back for analysis. I spit into the vial after eating carrots a few minutes before, and it turned the contents a light shade of orange. *Perhaps my results would say I was related to the carrot family*, I thought snarkily. I was supposed to do the test before the trip, like Billy did, but I was resisting doing this myself. At this point, I felt it was a waste of time and money. This didn't have anything to do with who I was, although my body was on edge. I felt like my soul was hurting, and what information I did have should have been good enough.

Several weeks later, I got my DNA results in an email. I waited a few days, not expecting any news beyond seeing my parents' names and family trees. When I finally settled into my home office chair and opened the email, I gasped: the test showed Billy and I only had half relatives in common, and only on our mom's side. We only had one parent in common.

What went wrong? It had to be the carrots, I thought. Could the carrots affect the DNA of my saliva and skew the result? I called the customer service line, thinking this must be a mistake.

"I ate carrots, so maybe that made it harder to read?" I asked the customer service rep.

"No, that wouldn't affect the results," she said. "We get this all the time. I know the information you may have learned is hard to accept, but the best thing you can do is communicate with your family. This is something you're going to have to work out with your loved ones." I hung up the phone, my ears ringing. None of this made sense.

I called Billy, who had taken the same DNA test to help with my ancestral healing assignment. Billy confirmed the dad listed on his DNA results was the one we both grew up with, along his side of the family. This dad wasn't on any of my DNA test results. Thelma was next on my call list. We always knew she had a different dad, and he played in a band with the dad on Billy's test results. I begged her to take the same test, on the off chance her dad was my biological dad. A couple of weeks later, Thelma got the results. We compared them to mine and it confirmed she and I were still half-siblings. Billy and I were not full siblings as we thought for our entire lives. Thelma and I were still half-siblings.

"Did you call mom?" Thelma asked.

I took a deep breath: I had to face Mom again.

A few afternoons later, I came home from work. I pulled up the test results on my computer and prepared to call Mom. A lump formed in my throat. For the entire day, I'd prepared for what might happen when I spoke to her again. Billy and I talked while I was at work, double and triple-checking the results and what the DNA company told us. We went through many different scenarios to determine the best way to get the truth from Mom.

My heart was racing so fast. I trembled as I made the call. Once we were both on the line, I took a deep breath and told her the results. At first, Mom bristled at what I was saying: that the dad I grew up with wasn't my biological father. That he only appeared on Billy's test results, not mine, proving I had no genetic link in common with the man I called dad for my entire life.

"Your dad is your dad," she insisted. "I wasn't with any other guys. I don't know why you're doing this to me."

"I've checked with everybody," I said.

"Those tests can be wrong," she said.

"No, it's not."

She hung up on me twice. I called back three times.

On the third call, she started to cry.

"I've never talked about this," she said. "but I'll tell you."

This was her story: my mom, Elise, was 17 years old when she gave birth to my sister Thelma. Grandma was helping Elise raise Thelma, and they were living together. She was underage, and Grandma felt she had authority over her. While Elise was trying to make her own decisions about her child, Grandma felt like a parent and had a say in how Thelma was raised. Elise was desperate to leave home with Thelma, so she took what savings she had and put money down on an apartment. The owner lived on the first floor and agreed to watch Thelma while my mom worked at a health insurance company during the day.

But my grandma had other plans. Hellbent on controlling her, she drained Elise's bank account, went over to her apartment and told the owner she was underage, and therefore couldn't rent her an apartment. Then she went to Elise's workplace and pulled her work permit, which caused her to lose her job. Then she found out where Elise was staying temporarily with Thelma. With three policemen flanking her, she ripped Thelma out of my mom's arms. Mom fell to the floor crying. She could have put up a fight in court, but she didn't have the money and resources to do so. Worse still, Mom had no way of supporting Thelma even if she could get her back.

Elise began drinking in a downward spiral until she passed out and broke out in hives. Somehow, she ended up in Atlantic City, New Jersey. She didn't remember how. All she knew was she was trying to drink herself to death in the wake of losing Thelma. She tried to survive by finding a job on the boardwalk go-go dancing in the evenings, donning a bolero vest and bell bottom pants—as was the groovy style of the late 1960's. Men would look for girls who were vulnerable and didn't appear to have families.

After dancing one night at the club, Elise went to dinner with a group of girls. Later that night, she found herself trapped in a basement apartment that reeked of cigar smoke and whiskey. She didn't know how she got there. There were several girls down there in a cramped space. There were little windows at the top of the apartment. She could see cracks of light coming out of the basement window, but there was no way for her to go through them to escape. The carpeting was stained, musty brown, and smelled like mold.

Most of the time, men shot the girls up with dope. If she or the other girls fought back, they'd get beaten, tied up, and raped. If one of them had to go to the bathroom while tied up for hours, they weren't allowed to get up. My mom's hair was matted as she was strapped to her bed. If the girls were "being good," according to this well-dressed man, they were let free. But when they left for the night, they would tie them up so they couldn't go anywhere.

One day, a girl in the bed near my mom's managed to free one of her hands from the rope, and then the other. When she freed herself, she untied Mom and wrapped a urine-soaked sheet around her naked body. They snuck into an alleyway in the back of the building. A kind security guard found them sitting and rocking on the curb, their arms around their knees. He contacted the police, who tried to call my grandmother, but there was no answer. Only Bill, my mom's good friend, answered the phone.

Bill sent money down for a bus ticket and picked my mom up at the bus station. She tried to tell him about her ordeal, but he didn't want to know.

"It's behind you," he said. "Don't ever think about it again."

When my mom came back home, she put the horrific experience far out of her mind. She married Bill and neither one of them said anything when they discovered Mom was pregnant. Bill was actually thrilled, proud that he was going to have a child. He doted on Elise, making sure she had what she needed. She seemed happy too. They were in love. They would love this baby together.

"Let's name her Angel if she's a girl," said Bill. "If it's a boy, we'll name him Bill."

Elise agreed. Even though the doctor's claimed she carried me for 10 months, Mom claimed she didn't have a second thought that the baby *wasn't* Bill's. She and Bill went on to have Billy and Paul, and she was reunited with Thelma after proving she was a fit mother to her grandmother. Mom believed with all of her heart that I was Bill's child, until fifty-two years later when I called her with these DNA results.

When Mom finished her story, I had trouble digesting the facts: she really believed she was 10 months pregnant? Why didn't her friend and her go to the police station after escaping? What sense did it make to wait in the alleyway? While my mom's storytelling left me with questions, one fact became clear: the dad I had known my whole life wasn't my biological father. It seemed I was actually the child of rape. Whether my mom truly believed she was 10 months pregnant or was doing what Bill suggested, putting it behind her, this was the truth. A pulsating part of me said she knew this from my conception, and the only one who was finding out this information for the first time was me. She'd never admit to that part of the story either way, and with her seeming deflection of the truth for as long as I could remember, there was no point in trying to prove when she knew I wasn't Bill's daughter.

I felt like I was floating above myself. While I stared at the results on my big computer screen, my feelings ran from sympathy, even empathy, to rage, and back again. I felt an overwhelming feeling for her, one a mother feels for her child. All I wanted to do in that moment was to hold her and protect her. It all made sense now. I had felt like an imposter, like a stranger, an enemy to this family. No wonder she treated me like this. Who would want someone like me around? I had this love for her, but hate for myself.

Her words sent my brain through a speeding rewind of my life. My memories zoomed past like a bullet train through a tunnel. I caught each of the most traumatic scenes of my life, remembering how she treated me, how she rejected me, how she couldn't love me. *She had to have known before she told me this story today*, I thought.

Rocking me when I was three years old, my mother almost dropped me over the banister of the stairs. I kept thinking she was going to throw me over it. This was my earliest memory. I had the sense she was going to drop me, and yet it's the only time I remember her hugging me. Did this happen because I reminded her of her horrifying ordeal in Atlantic City?

This had to be why Mom treated me as she did all these years. My biological father, whoever he was, intended to hurt my mother—perhaps kill her—and I was the byproduct of that violence. The words seeped into this swirling carousel of memories. I wondered what it all meant, the choices I'd made, and the way I was made to feel about myself and others. Could I forgive my mother for not telling me until now?

Chapter 2

On Dunkle Street, in the inner city of Harrisburg, Pennsylvania, I rode my bike everywhere. It was an old school cruiser with a banana-colored seat and big, long handlebars. I'd wiggle the handles, make them loose at the bottom or adjust them up high, biker style.

This was my freedom in 1974 as a seven-year-old who never wanted to be home, zipping around town, and always with somewhere else to go.

As soon as I woke up on an almost-start-of-summer day, I had my mind set on getting my feet onto those silver pedals. I threw on a yellow tank top with white shorts, although my shorts would get covered in dirt by the end of the day. Half the time, I ran around barefoot, being your typical Tom Sawyer-like kid. I'd stepped on a nail one time and needed to have a tetanus shot, but I still continued going out barefoot.

I didn't hate wearing shoes: I simply couldn't find them in my room most mornings, let alone tie the laces. Sometimes I rescued them from under bags of clothes and piles of trash in my house, other times I'd find two from different pairs. Kids teased me when I came to school like that, but I didn't have a choice. In the summer, I was just glad to be outside.

Billy, Paul, Thelma, and I grabbed two pieces of toast each, which had been donated to us from a local shelter, before we headed outside. I caught a brief glimpse of Mom. She was putting food on the porch banisters to feed the squirrels in front of our house. She loved watching them eat. My last image before I left for the day was the back of her dark, shoulder-length hair.

Once on the street, I reveled in how the warm sunshine felt on my shoulders as I rode, hands-free, down this great big hill. I felt the wind in my face. I was ready to explore. I found a bird's nest, looked under rocks, and collected lizards and salamanders to later hide under my bed in a container. I caught up with my brothers and we'd go on adventures in the neighborhood.

"Let's go look at empty houses!" I said. We rode our bikes to each of them, pretending ghosts were inside and playing hide-and-seek. We explored neighborhoods nearby, and made friends wherever we went. We did this for hours. In the waning dusk, we played kick-the-can in the middle of the street until we were the only kids still running around outside.

Everyone's parents screamed out their windows for them to come home. Except our Mom. She didn't call for us.

It was 9:00 p.m.

We looked at each other and thought we better head back.

At the end of the school year, I was standing at the bus stop with a few high schoolers who were balancing something furry and small in their hands. All the kids were gathered around. I looked and saw a baby squirrel.

"Where did you get it?" I asked.

"My dog got into the nest and killed the babies," said one of the teenage boys. "I'm going to give it to the science teacher."

A burning feeling overcame my body. This little creature could become part of a dissection demonstration. I had to rescue that squirrel, feeling a sense of determination.

"Please, can I have it?" I asked, begging. "My mom loves squirrels, and she'll take care of it." I put my hand on his arm, not letting him go. Exhausted from my begging, he handed the squirrel to me wrapped in a hand towel.

When I got home, I presented the squirrel to Mom. She was so excited.

"Oh my god, where did you find her?" she said, mesmerized, grabbing the squirrel who chattered away. She immediately named her Chatty and went to grab a dropper to feed her water. She went about the kitchen trying to figure out how to smash nuts in the water so she could feed the baby easily. I finally felt important; *I* was the one who got her this beloved squirrel. Although she didn't seem to love me, I felt it through the squirrel.

But Thelma didn't feel that way, Chatty was just another obstacle to us receiving love from our mom, and complained about the little squirrel the moment she came into the house.

Mom handed Chatty to her partner. No, not Bill. He was long gone from our home, which had devolved into screaming matches after I was born. He was furious that Mom was cheating on him, and he finally left when I was three years old. I barely saw him after that. Mom ended up moving the object of her affair into our home, a woman named Louise. Soft and kind, Louise changed the whole energy of the house. She seemed to be everything Mom wanted, a partner who took care of the little things and held her together. Mom looked at her with warm eyes as she passed Chatty into her arms. Louise returned the gaze with the same intensity as their fingers touched. She gave Chatty fresh water and food every day, doting on her like a child.

Chatty ended up inheriting the same size room as my sister and me, except our shared room was in the attic and often filled with trash and unwashed sheets. Chatty enjoyed a huge cage that was like a little sanctuary, and Mom always kept it clean.

Another morning, I was trying to sneak out of the house because Mom didn't like being disturbed. I was tiptoeing around to find my shoes and something to eat. She was sitting at the kitchen table and painting ceramics by herself. No hug "goodbye" before I left, or a stern but loving, "Have fun, but be sure you're home in time for dinner." The last thing I saw of her was the back of her head as I left through the front door, her paintbrush in motion, adding the finishing touches on an elephant. Her purse lay on a table in the foyer, where her food stamps poked out of her wallet.

It didn't seem like Mom worked a regular job, but her creative way of making money was finding other things to do. While we lived off of welfare, she would make extra money painting ceramics, washing dogs, and baking cakes. But these efforts didn't pay all of the bills, and my mom moved a total of 18 times during my childhood. The house on Dunkle Street was number eight, and would be the last time I moved with my mom.

After riding around for the day, my brothers, Louise's son, Scott, and I were sitting outside our house. Scott was lanky with big brown eyes, a pale—almost pure white—complexion, and a crown of puffy, big-locked curls. He looked at me the same way he always did before daring me to do something. He clasped his hands together and wrung them around. His mind seemed to be working overtime. He knew I was adventurous, so this had to be a good one. We were sitting outside our house while Mom left Chatty and her ceramics to throw our old mattresses over the balcony. My mattress reeked of pee. I was the only one of the kids who peed the bed regularly. It infuriated my mom, so much so she decided not to put sheets on my bed anymore or she'd toss out my mattress like she did this afternoon.

The mattress landed with a thud in the backyard.

"I dare you to jump from the balcony onto the mattresses," he said.

I didn't flinch. Once my mom was back inside the house, I climbed on top of the balcony, bent my knees and took a running leap. I fell flat on my old mattress, getting a dizzying nose-full of urine. The muffled cheers from Scott and my brothers made the leap, and the stench, worth it.

Later that evening, Thelma and I got ready for bed. We had to share her mattress since mine had been thrown out earlier that day. We sat and talked, and tickled each other. She read from one of her latest *Nancy Drew* books, and handed me a cartoon to work on from her *Draw Me* pamphlet. As she watched me play, she asked, "Instead of running around tomorrow, why don't you help me clean the house?"

"OK," I said, "But you never come outside and play with me. Will you help me catch salamanders tomorrow, and I promise I'll help you clean?"

"Deal," she said.

We drifted asleep talking about our day. When Thelma was completely asleep, I woke up and felt that familiar tingle, but I stayed in bed because every time I got up to use the restroom, something bad would happen to me. Mom's visitors would come to my house and touch me. They would force me to go down on them. I'd stuff toilet paper in my mouth to blot out the taste. If I was watching TV with them, they would make me touch their private parts. Whether or not it was an adult I thought I could trust, I feared getting up to go to the bathroom and hearing that doorknob turn. I would leap up and squeeze my body under the claw tub to hide.

The door would open.

"I know you're in here," the adult would say. "Are you trying to hide from me?"

I couldn't stop him. I had to endure the experience.

As I laid in bed, I let the urine flow out of me and onto the mattress, and it had almost become a natural thing to do at this point. I was frozen in place.

My mind kept telling me if I stayed in bed, even if I had to go pee, nothing bad would ever happen to me. I didn't want to keep being an easy target for my mom's friends.

The next morning, I tried to cover the yellow stain on Thelma's mattress with my blanket. But when Thelma woke up, she could see and smell I had an accident in bed. Not wanting to tell Mom and make her angry at me, she knew a bike ride would get me out of the house.

"Just go out on the bike for a while," she said. "If you don't get home before it's dark, though, I won't help you catch salamanders next time!"

"OK, Thelma!" I said.

I quietly walked down the steps, eager to get on my bike and make my usual rounds in the neighborhood. In the living room, my mom stood silently. No ceramics. No Chatty. Just staring. At me. Someone else was there too, her friend, Jeffrey. I overheard Mom saying he just got out of prison for killing someone. I was frightened. He was a tall, robust black man with a high afro with the sides squashed on either side. I didn't really know him, or why Mom was hanging around him.

"You better not have peed on Thelma's mattress," my mom said. Her arms were crossed and her expression hard. Calculating. Cold. It was hard enough for me to form words and speak on a regular day, but when my mom confronted me, I had no idea how to respond.

"Tell me," she said. "I can go upstairs and look for myself."

I didn't answer. This made her fly into a rage.

"I got this, Elise," said Jeffrey. He grabbed my arm.

"I don't know you!" I screamed, tears rolling down my face. I was hyperventilating. My mom was always threatening to send me away, and now she was going to have someone beat me. Jeffrey lifted me by my arm and dragged me up the stairs. Mom seemed happy to see me, the kid who rode her bike around the neighborhood and made all of her friends on her own, was afraid of somebody. Watching me squirm seemed to bring Mom and Jeffrey a perverse joy.

Once Jeffrey dragged me to my room, he undid his belt, and I figured he would simply beat me as my mom had. But then he unzipped his pants. I left my body, realizing this was like so many times before. The nightmares I envisioned, the reason I didn't leave my bed at night. In this moment with Jeffrey, I wished I didn't recognize this feeling all too well, and how easily I escaped from my own body. This was not the first time this would happen to me, and unfortunately wouldn't be the last.

Riding my bike to school was no longer my only escape from being touched. My carefree nature began to clash with the burning, growing well of anger inside of me. I no longer felt like Harrisburg was my stomping ground. Instead of going door-to-door singing songs from church to earn money for soda, candy, and kites, I started stealing. No longer was I satisfied with only getting clothes from Goodwill and other charity organizations. I could just take what I wanted.

One day before school, I found Mom's food stamps in her purse. If she was getting them for free, I could have them for free. I had heard Mom saying because she had four kids, she could have more of them. In my mind,

I thought of everything literally. Why wouldn't she let me have them if they were for me?

At school on our lunch break, I held up the food stamps.

"Who wants to get candy?" I shouted in the cafeteria.

As it turned out, *everyone* wanted candy. The other kids and I stampeded out of the school's double doors and down its cascade of steps.

At the candy store, with its glass display case of penny candy, and the bigger candy behind the counter, I felt like the queen of the school. I lead this mob to Sugar Daddies, Charleston Chews, Snickers, and Hershey Bars. The selection was not the usual penny candy. We were going for the good stuff.

I handed kids fives and tens, encouraging them to get whatever they wanted. The rowdy line was out the door of the store. Kids screamed their orders at the visibly overwhelmed shop-keep, and ran back to school with armloads of candy instead of going to the cafeteria for lunch.

But I hadn't foreseen one part of my plan: getting back without running into trouble. The principal saw all of us running back to school holding the candy. The jig was almost up.

As I rode to school on my bike the next day, rumors were starting. Angel was loaded with a fistful of food stamps, they said, and she was giving it to her classmates for candy. The kids were calling it "paper food money." The rumors got up to the principal, and he called Mom. She confirmed her food stamps had been stolen. The principal called the police, who were going to greet me before my first class began.

"Angel, I need to see you," the principal urged as I walked down the hall. I followed him to his office. Two officers stood side-by-side with their hands on their belts.

"Did you steal your mom's food stamps?" one of the officers asked. I thought they were going to take me away; I felt like a ticking time bomb. It was too bad I couldn't use my usual go-to tough line to get out of this one: *I'll bite you. I'll just bite you.* It was my usual escape route from bullying at home and school. I was wriggling in the police's net for stealing Mom's food stamps. She wasn't going to forgive me, much less understand why I did it.

The police told my mom to take care of me, and to consider this my first warning. When I got home, Mom railed against me. I wished for the days when she would ignore me and pay attention to Chatty or her ceramics. I stood there, still smelling like pee and wearing two mismatched shoes with knots in the back of my head because I hadn't had time to take a bath before school. There was always talk about me behind my back. Kids called me the "pissy girl." The school would often send me home with clothes and connect me with social services. But the police officers didn't do anything.

When I got home, Mom started pacing the floor. She knew her children could be taken away, and the police officers not doing anything today bought her time. Secretly, she knew she was not only going to potentially lose me, but my brothers and Thelma, if she didn't find a safer place for us to go. Instead of being transparent about her fears, she instilled the fear in us instead.

"Go to your room," said Mom. "We are gonna have to figure out what to do with you."

"Moms love their kids," I said. "Moms are there for their kids!"

Mom shook her head. "I don't know what I'm going to do with you."

"I hate you! I'm going to go someplace where somebody loves me."

"That's it," she said. "I'm taking your bike away."

My one prized possession. My freedom.

"You're getting into nothing but trouble," she continued. "Where's the bike? Louise, take the bike and put it in the basement."

"You can't take my bike away!" I said. I could have tried apologizing, but my rage bubbled over. There was no stopping my torrent of words and kicks.

Louise brought it in from the outside.

"There are plenty of kids at work who will want it," Mom said, with a stern look on her face. Desperate, I lunged at Mom, kicking and screaming, but stopped myself short of grabbing her. I was too afraid I'd get beat with a belt buckle. I retreated upstairs and went into my room. I grabbed my single mattress, light enough for me to throw through the open window. I hurled it down the second floor, watching it land from my room.

I kicked, rocked, and screamed, "I. Hate. Mom. I. Hate. Mom."

Without my bike, I was late for school the next day. As I began walking the one mile to school, I saw one leaning on the wall of the corner store in my neighborhood. *I could borrow it and bring it back before anyone noticed*, I thought. I brought up the right peddle and started riding. I threw down the bike outside of school and ran inside. When the owner reported the bike as stolen, the principal confirmed I took the bike to school. The police saw the bike at the school steps, and confirmed it matched the owner's description.

When they talked to the principal, he confirmed he saw me drop the bike and run inside to get a hall pass since I was late.

The police called Mom and said she had to pick me up from school. When we came home, she launched into her usual routine of saying, "I'm sick and I can't handle you anymore, Angel." She threatened to send me away to a school for children to live in. "Well, that's it," she continued. "I'm sending you away."

Suddenly, my life began drifting away. Riding my bike. Taking the dares from Scott. Catching salamanders. I didn't speak often, but I had to at least go on record.

"Everyone else's mom is there for them," I said, strong—yet shaking inside. "I don't even have shoes. Moms wake up. Moms make their kids breakfast. Moms clean the house."

Mom had no reaction, no feeling about it. She'd already made up her mind.

Mom tried to take me to a Christian home for children, but I couldn't go because I had too many disciplinary actions against me at my old school. They didn't feel like they could handle me. Then she asked a psychiatrist about any homes they had. They gave her a pamphlet about Scotland School. The school was exclusively for veteran's children, and since Bill had fought in Vietnam, I was eligible to go. It seemed like the right choice, at least Mom thought so. Mom sent Thelma to Milton Hershey School since she had a different dad who wasn't a veteran.

As she drove my brothers and me to Scotland School, I wondered what I'd do every day. I hadn't wanted to leave the life I created for myself on Dunkle Street. Poor Thelma was many miles away and could only be sad and fearful for me. I know she would have looked over me if she could. But a growing part of me was relieved to not live with Mom anymore. I didn't have to keep living with a woman who didn't love me, or invited over strangers who hurt me.

Mom dropped us off at Scotland School. She hugged and kissed my brothers goodbye. She didn't hug or kiss me goodbye, so I stood off to the side. As she drove away, my brothers and I looked around. Most of the people looked super big and we looked so small. Would we fit in? "Don't worry, I'll protect you," I said. The campus looked beautiful. I was thinking about how I could explore it. The grass was green and manicured. It was June sixth, three days after my eighth birthday.

A new kind of feeling washed over me: *relief.*

The bad things that were happening to me in my house would stop.

We shared a room with four people in homes called cottages. Beds were made with all four corners tucked in. We all had chores. We had new, clean clothes from the school and we stitched our names into them. They fit us all. These clothes were donated from the community. We didn't have toothbrushes growing up, and it was good to have them. It felt good to have hot showers after life with only cold baths. Whether this change would help or harm me, I would find out. For now, I had a clean room and clean clothes. Still, I yearned for the summer days when my bike took me far away from my pain.

Chapter 3

After a couple of weeks at my new school, I still thought about my bike. I missed the adventures I took on Dunkle Street until 9:00 p.m. and the dares that went un-dared with Scott. It was fall, and my old friends and classmates were probably back on a regular school schedule. The times where I freely roamed my neighborhood were replaced with a healthier structure, far better than life in Mom's house. Even though I felt safer here, I was also stuck inside of a chain-link fence and limited in where I could walk and explore within the campus. Plus, I missed Thelma, so I had to busy myself with new activities. I sang in the choir. I got whatever I wanted with the pocket money they gave me, like a twenty-five cent candy bar without scheming to steal my mom's food stamps and sending my classmates stampeding out of the cafeteria. My new classmates and I had movie nights with free popcorn and snacks.

Here, I was a normal child for the most part, even though I couldn't escape the big red letter F on my homework or tests in my classes. No one knew why my grades were so bad. All I knew was words looked like a blur on the page, or shapes I couldn't pronounce or write. Back in Harrisburg, I was always in special help and didn't speak much in my classes. I tried to do better at Scotland School, but the same pattern followed me into my new life.

My math teacher, Mrs. Moore, gave out our latest graded test. As she put mine on my desk, she gave me an extra-long look as she caught me twirling my hair and staring outside at the tire swing in the playground. I was captivated by how the swing swayed between the trees.

"Angel," my teacher said, in an attempt to get my head out of the clouds.

I looked down at the F and couldn't understand my own handwriting. I didn't seem to be getting it, and in this wonderful place with clean clothes and sheets and movie nights, this part of my life—the part with learning— was still stagnant, unmoving. I twirled my long bangs between my fingers and pretended I understood what Mrs. Moore was telling the class. As long as I didn't ask questions, maybe they wouldn't realize I wasn't understanding the lessons, even though I loved asking random questions.

"How do you do your hair?" I asked Mrs. Moore.

"We're talking about math right now," she replied.

Outside of math class, Mrs. Moore saw how I was brash and fun, spinning on the tire swing and making friends easily. I excelled in art class, where I painted with a deep passion and used my paintbrush as a gateway to an untapped part of myself. That's when she sat me down and made me listen to calming cassettes, which I called "sandman" cassettes. They filled my ears and mind with sounds of the ocean. She even cut my bangs to see if not having them meant I'd stop twirling them and start paying attention. That didn't happen. She tried to teach me how to tie my shoes since I kept running around with them untied—or with no shoes at all. No amount of cassettes with ocean sounds, or cutting my bangs, or tying my shoes would make me pay more attention in class. I knew other teachers were talking about me.

"She needs to be smart enough to tie her shoes," Mrs. Moore said to Mr. Gomez in the hallway, not realizing I was eavesdropping nearby.

"Maybe we can get her diagnosed," Mr. Gomez said.

Before the end of the school year, I was diagnosed with ADHD and dyslexia.

I didn't know what that meant, except for the fact they started me on medicine for ADHD. And I still had to listen to those sleepy cassettes.

Summer came. Mom was going to pick us up. I could see the light through trees, see Scott warming up to make a new dare. We were all ready to go home.

Billy, Paul, and I waited in the carpool line. My mom rolled up in the passenger seat of a 1978 dark blue Ford LTD. By this time, Louise had left Mom, but that didn't mean Mom was lonely for long. In the driver's seat was her new girlfriend, Bernie, a woman Mom had met at the bar and started living with. I met Bernie before we left for Scotland School, when I had to go to the local bar at night to retrieve Mom. They had a Schnauzer dog hanging out of the window named Turkey. Billy and Paul opened the passenger door and piled in, but when I tried to get in, my mom said, "Boys, shut the door."

Confused, I started shaking. Why couldn't I get in the car? She started the car engine, and locked the door. I didn't understand what was happening.

"Sorry, Angel," she said, shaking her head. "You'll be staying here for the summer because your grades are terrible."

"But I want to go home!" I screamed, throwing a tantrum.

"C'mon boys," she said as my brothers buckled their seatbelts. They looked helplessly out the window, too young and too scared to speak up for me.

"I hate you!" I yelled at Mom, and kicked her rear tire. I picked up a rock and threw it at the car as she drove away. I ran back to my cottage and started rocking in my room. I felt so alone, so abandoned. I couldn't believe she was leaving me. As I watched most of the other kids pile into their parents' cars, I wondered how many of us would be left over the summer. I went back into the deserted hallway, without the bustling of my friends having to get to class or the cafeteria or complete our chores.

Although Mom said she left me at school because of my bad grades, I wasn't put into summer school to work on getting A's and B's. In fact, I wasn't going to get extra math help either. I was simply left, it seemed, as a punishment. Did I need those classes, or had my mom just said that as an excuse to leave me here over the summer?

Without the hope of Mom picking me up to spend Christmas with Thelma and my brothers, I would have to figure out my own plans. A flyer in one of the community rooms touted the school's upcoming holiday show, where students could write and act in skits, play instruments, and sing onstage. The kids who performed would each get to pick three gifts from the American Legion catalog. Feeling a jolt of excitement, I planned to play the flute and act out scenes in the show since I was taking flute in music class. I unfolded my stand so I could memorize "Oh, Holy Night" and "Hark! The Herald Angels Sing." One of my friends sang the songs as I played the flute.

After our performance, I felt my whole heart pounding with excitement during the last ovation. I knew what would happen next. One of the matrons handed me a gift-wrapped present, and I immediately tore into it. Inside was the answer to my American Legion gift form: a choice of three different kinds of recorders, one of them being a sing-along recorder, which is the one I picked. I gasped, thrilled at my new connection to music, and the freedom I could experience while listening to my favorite songs.

As winter turned into spring and then summer, I spent most of my time swinging under the sunlight that shone through the leaves on the trees, listening to James Taylor songs on my tape recorder over and over again. I accepted the reality that Mom wouldn't come to get me. Then, I had a thought that hadn't crossed my mind in awhile: would Dad come save me?

Sure, I barely saw him, but if he'd seen how Mom was treating me this year, he'd do something. He just had to. I decided Dad *would* come and get me someday. He'd rescue me from being all alone and struggling in school. In the quiet of the afternoon, I chanted, "Dad's gonna rescue me, Dad's gonna rescue me." I imagined my father, with his dark features and charismatic smile, driving up to take me away. I'd hop in and spend the whole summer with him. Just him and me.

But instead, I was here, with only my tapes to keep me company. I twirled on the tire swing and sang to myself to get my imagination going. I looked to the sky and made my own dare, not with a person but whoever was watching over me, who would be the friend I needed.

God, if you're real, wake me up at 2:00 a.m. tonight.

At 2:00 a.m., I startled awake, laying in the white sheets of my bed, shaking, a little nervous, but also feeling powerful. *He'd done it!* God actually awakened me when I asked him to. *Alright, God, how do I know if this is a fluke or not? How do I know you're for real?* Let's try this again: *if you're really real, God, wake me up at 3:00 a.m. tomorrow night.*

The next morning at 3:00 a.m., I startled awake as I had the night before. This time, feeling more confident, I walked into the darkened hallway and double-checked the digital clock. It blinked at 3:00 a.m.

God was here.

Although Mom had left me and, I'm sure, Dad was still figuring out a good time to save me, God would be my new best friend. I imagined him as this Santa Claus-like man with a big white beard and pure white hair. Suddenly, it was OK my mom wasn't here.

It was OK she didn't take me home for the summer.

It was OK when kids got calls from their parents and I didn't get one.

I had this new relationship with God.

On the swing the next day, I listened to Stevie Wonder's song, "Have a Talk with God."

I talked to God all day.

Thelma knew about my troubles in school, including my illegible handwriting. She still wanted to talk with me over the summer. We were separated for long stretches of time.

In her own way, Thelma was trying to keep me learning at school while watching over me. We weren't allowed to call other kids. There was a list of contacts, and the number coming in had to come from a number that came from our parents. We were only allowed to receive calls. This made it harder to talk to Thelma.

"Wait, what about the tape recorder you got at school for Christmas?" she asked. Her scheme was to start sending me tapes. "I'm going to send you tapes so you can send them back," she added. "Just don't break the tabs."

This way, we could keep the same tape going back-and-forth.

When I received her first one, I clutched it as if it was gold, like Charlie Bucket did when he found the golden ticket in *Willy Wonka and the Chocolate Factory*. I closed the door to the bedroom I shared with four other kids, and carefully put the cassette in my tape recorder and hit "play." Thelma's voice began pinging off the walls, instantly comforting me, soothing me. My big sister, three years older than me, was more like my mom than my actual mom.

This was the best way to do it because I couldn't write.

"We went to Hershey Park," she said on one tape, and she described what it looked like, what she did that day, what our brothers were doing with her.

"I roller skated down a hill and broke my arm," I recorded.

I sang from Michael Jackson's *Off the Wall*. We both loved "I Will Survive" by Gloria Gaynor.

"Oh my god, Peaches and Herb came to Milton Hershey School," she told me in a high, excited voice on one tape. I sent back my rendition of "Reunited."

It was the dialogue of our lives.

One day, I ran out of tapes. Since I was looking in the mail every day for my sister to send the tapes back, I had gotten impatient and was trying to figure out how to get the money to buy more tapes from school. At this point, I'd been moved to Cottage Thirty-three. Some of the other kids left over for the summer started giving me a hard time. I was trying to get back to my room when one of them blocked the doorway. I moved from side-to-side, but she moved along with me. Her name was Margarita, and she was tall with dry, cracked skin on her hands.

"Let her get by," said a strong voice from behind me. I looked around, and saw a stone-faced girl in jeans, a white collared shirt and an afro. Margarita immediately moved. It turns out she was afraid of my brazen new ally.

"Hey, I'm Tanya," she said, extending her hand and breaking into a grin. A handshake seemed a little mature for a 10-year-old kid who was only one year older than me, but I shook her hand anyway. She had dark skin, soft, brown eyes, chunky cheeks and when she wasn't smiling, she looked like you should fear her.

"Are you looking for something?" she asked.

"More tapes," I said.

"For what?"

"I send tapes back-and-forth with my sister. My mom left me here."

"I have summer school this year," she said, her face falling, but only for a moment. "But I might be able to help you with the tapes," she added.

Tanya somehow convinced her mom to send her money for tapes. Whether her mom knew what the money was for or not, I had no idea. I let her in on the tapes Thelma had been sending me. Tanya actually wanted to contribute songs and story ideas to the compilations to the tapes.

"Tanya, look at this!" I'd say when a new tape from Thelma came in the mail.

Like a duck imprinting on her mom, I followed Tanya everywhere, and she had the feet to match: her feet stuck out to the left and right. I would walk behind her, because I thought if I did, then I would be like her. She was the Punky Brewster to my Pippi Longstocking.

That summer, Tanya was almost pulled out of school to take care of her mom. In her own way, she was glad to stay here and keep being a kid. She had the opposite problem of me where her mom *needed* her as a guardian, and Mom didn't need me for anything.

Tanya wanted to adopt me, and tried to get her mom to take me home when she called her once a week. She did everything she could to protect me. While her mom never adopted me, she bought tapes, candy, and shampoo because I was always using Tanya's, who would cornrow my hair, and it was beautiful. The shampoo was a welcome break from the effective, but basic, military surplus soap we used at school for everything from showers to handwashing.

My usual swing time in the afternoon spilled into the evenings with Tanya. At nighttime, we explored the underground tunnels, and used flares to check out the fallout shelters. Around 1:00 or 2:00 a.m., we would sneak outside to run and swim through water particles, like a mist cloud. We stood on the hill, watching the clouds gather in its hollow. This was a usual sight in the gullies of Pennsylvania. They felt like real clouds, which you could move and sway around with your fingers. We felt like we were in heaven. It was a moment I got to play with both of my friends at school: Tanya and God. The quiet of the grounds told me He was listening, He was tagging along on our adventures. We'd usually end the evening by sneaking into unlocked cottages and smoking cigarettes, making clouds of nicotine instead of water. When I felt sad, Tanya put a hand on my shoulder and said, "Don't worry, your dad will come get you."

Over the next few years, I filled my time not only with my beloved tape recorder, but adventures with Tanya. One summer, Tanya and I went to Camp Legion, where we played softball until the sun set, caught salamanders, competed in watermelon eating contests, and took polar dips in the lake every morning. The years melted away as easily as Rocket popsicles in Tanya's and my hot hands. I was doing what I loved full-time.

When I finally visited my family for the summer or a holiday, it was mostly with my grandmother, Dad's mom. If I couldn't be with Dad, who lived in Texas, at least I could spend time with the next best thing: Grandma. She would welcome me in the kitchen, all five-foot-zero of her with frizzy, dark hair; dark complexion; big brown eyes; a soft, broad nose; and a warm, wide smile.

She'd take me to Buffalo State Park in Perry County, which had been owned by Dad's family for generations. There was a family graveyard here, which they willed to the state park as long as the park didn't disturb those plots. Grandma took me to the graveyard and told me stories about our roots. Every time Grandma and I visited, she came armed with a patient answer every time I asked about Dad and his new wife, Sheree.

"Did you tell him what we did today?" I'd ask after we left the graveyard.

"Of course, sweetie," she'd say, and continue telling my stories about our family.

Five years after Mom left me at school or I was at Grandma's house for the summer, I headed into my eighth-grade year. I still asked God to bring Dad to me. I lived every day the best I could, but it became my ultimate dream to spend time with him. The morning after Tanya's and my latest adventure in the mist, one of the matrons of the school told me to pack up my things.

"Your dad is coming to get you," she said.

I shrieked with joy. It was really happening! Apparently, Grandma convinced him to move back and live with her. She told him how my brothers, Thelma and I had been living in homes, and it seemed he wanted to come take us out of school. God really was listening!

Tanya helped me put my things in a bag, including shampoo, my tapes, and my recorder. I gave her one of the tapes, and she grasped it.

"We'll still talk to each other," she said. "It's going to be OK."

I nodded, smiling. I was used to moving on, but Tanya's eyes were watery.

Stepping outside, I saw Dad in the driver's seat of his old blue pickup truck. Paul and Billy were there too with their backpacks, and they crammed into the backseat. Someone else I barely recognized was sitting in the passenger's seat. As I walked closer to the car, I could see it was this stepmom Grandma had mentioned: Sheree.

Through the window, Sheree didn't smile at me. She had dirty blonde, wavy hair and huge bug-like eyes, and she wore a flannel shirt and faded jeans. Dad had on a button up shirt and jeans. Even though he was actually short, in my mind he was really big.

Sitting in between the two of them as we drove, I felt as if I'd arrived. I had waited so long for this moment, just me and Dad and—well—Sheree was there too, but that was fine. I had most of what I wanted. For almost the entire drive, my eyes locked onto Dad's face, his ash brown hair, his beautiful dark skin and his light eyes. We listened to "Carolina in My Mind" by James Taylor over and over again. I hugged him and kissed his cheek, in total awe.

God had answered my prayers.

But I could feel the tension in Sheree as I stared at my dad. I could feel her eyes trained on the back of my head. As I hugged Dad, she began to churn in her seat.

"Stop it, Angel, he's gonna wreck," she said. "You gotta let him drive."

During the two-hour drive home, I ignored Sheree in the nicest way I could. I was on my way to salvation, along with my best friend, God. Plus,

I'd still keep in touch with Tanya. Everything was working out for me.

Or so I thought.

Chapter 4

The night I arrived at my new home, Dad and Sheree shut the door to their bedroom. They thought I was asleep, but I could hear the yells through the wall. "She's too old to be all over you," Sheree said, talking about the drive from Scotland School. "No teenager should be hanging on their dad like that. It's not healthy."

I held my breath, waiting for Dad to speak up for me, to say, "She's my daughter and I love her, and that's the end of it." But he didn't say that. All I heard was silence.

The next day, I said good morning to Dad and reached out to give him a hug. He didn't look me in the eyes. Instead, he looked down and patted me on the shoulder. A few hours later, he took my twin brothers out to play with BB guns, but he didn't plan anything for him and me to do together. That set up the pattern from then on out. I'd see him in the kitchen for breakfast because we both ate at 7:30 a.m. before I went to school. But that was it. My hero was fading into a shadow as we passed each other in the hallways.

Sheree seemed to pick up where Dad left off, as if to keep an eye on me, so I wouldn't get too close to her husband. She drove me to the store to buy a few items for my bathroom and bedroom. A cigarette dangled from her mouth as she kept her eyes trained on the road. We drove without speaking until she finally started talking about a topic she'd harp on for years to come.

"You know, I had to save your dad from your mom," she said. "He was a mess without me."

I couldn't argue that Mom was hard to live with, but Sheree took it too far when she ended her tirade with, "Your mom is a horrible person."

Despite all I'd experienced with Mom, I still wasn't ready to say she was horrible. I may have said I hated her, may have kicked the tires as she drove away, but I was her daughter. I could say those things. She was still my mom.

Who was Sheree to say my mom was a horrible person?

Dad and Sheree lived with Grandma in Perry County, a pure country area with roads flanked by fields, cows, and farms that were dotted with red and white barns. It was worlds away from Scotland School, where friends like Tanya were the norm. At my new school, the only diversity was the type of plaid shirts each student wore. At West Perry, I sported my usual cornrows, shirt with sewn gold lines and baggy pants while everyone else was in flannel with cigarettes rolled up their sleeves. I'd taken on the style and culture of Scotland School, so among the predominantly white students, I stood out.

While I kept in touch with Tanya and Thelma, passing tapes back-and-forth through the mail, I had a new partner-in-mischief: Joann, a beautiful, brown-eyed blonde with a cheerful smile. We would go shopping, talk all afternoon, take dares, and sneak off to the bathroom to smoke. I'd hold the door as Joann took a few hits from her cigarette. If a teacher approached, I'd let go of the stall door, signaling to Joann she needed to toss her cigarette into the toilet. No smoke smell, no evidence.

One time, Joann gently grabbed a lock of my hair when she came out of the stall, twirling it in her fingers. "Have you ever thought about getting highlights?" she asked.

I shrugged. "I don't know how I'd sneak hair dye into my house."

"You don't need the stuff in a box," she said. "I'll show you. It'll look great."

After school that Friday, we went over to Grandma's house, knowing Sheree and Dad were out at a party together for the weekend. The only person we'd see was Grandma, who was retired from the Navy Depot and had time to work in her garden, tending to her tomatoes and peas. We found her eating a tomato and mayo sandwich, looking out the window. She was excited for me to dye my hair, watching Joann get lemons out of the fridge.

Joann helped me put lemon in my hair to lighten it up. As the juice set in, we sat on the back porch overlooking the apple trees, weeping willows, and oaks, gossiping about our classmates at school.

The next morning, I peered at my hair in the bathroom mirror. The streaks of beach blonde in my light brown hair framed my face, and I couldn't stop touching it. Joann looked pleased with the results, nodding and smiling. Her ride came, so she gave me a hug and left.

A few minutes later, I heard keys in the lock, and the loud shrillness of Sheree's voice pierced the air. Grandma had already retreated to her bedroom and shut the door. Sheree saw me in the bathroom as she walked by. She was still in her jeans and long, red nails—the old-fashioned acrylic ones from the drug store. Her mascara was smeared. I knew these were no ordinary parties;

I could smell the unmistakable whiff of marijuana on her jacket. Dad must've played music that night along with the party goers, who were usually 20 years younger than him.

Sheree turned on her heel to get another look at me.

"You look like a whore," she snapped.

She told me to get into the car. My fear of getting kicked out of the house compelled me to follow her. We were going to her friend's, she said, about a twenty-minute drive away. As it came into view, I saw it was an old, dug-in brown house with glass doors in the front. Sheree's friend, it seemed, was a hairstylist. We entered her home through the side of the house.

"I need you to help me out," Sheree demanded. "We need to get her hair back to her original color, or at least close. I don't want her walking around with these highlights."

"OK, what color?" asked her friend, Melissa.

"Dye it black," said Sheree, causing a wave of fear within me. I started to sob.

"Don't worry, you'll love it," said Melissa.

I couldn't breathe while Melissa began mixing the color together, and then washed and towel-dried my hair. My scalp burned. Sheree looked on, smoking a cigarette. The ordeal seemed to take hours. Melissa was kind and knitted her eyebrows together, realizing she was causing me pain, but she was also helpless to do anything about it with Sheree watching.

"Don't worry baby, it's gonna look pretty," Melissa kept saying.

"Yeah, but it's my hair," I said through hysterical tears. "She can't do this." I could hardly catch my breath since I was hyperventilating. The smell of the chemicals and my horror made me feel like I was going to pass out. I felt like I needed one of my mom's brown paper bags to breathe into. Sheree gave me a sharp glance, allowing my terror to continue.

When it was all over, I had charcoal black hair. The person staring back at me in the mirror looked like one of the goth kids in school. I'd seen them, but I didn't know them. Maybe I was going to fit into a crowd of kids at school I'd never known. My skin was so white against the deep black of my hair. I looked away; it became unbearable to keep looking in the mirror.

Sheree seemed satisfied, looking at the hair color and talking to Melissa about the party she and Dad both went to the night before.

Fearing I would be sent back to school, I didn't want to do anything wrong, not even to say how much this hair color disturbed me. Although Dad wasn't giving me attention, I wanted to stay here. What would I do now if I was sent back to Scotland School?

"How does it feel to be back to your natural color?" asked Sheree, driving us home.

"This isn't my natural hair color," I said. "My hair is brown!"

"We had to get all the light out of your hair," she said.

The next day, Dad saw my hair during breakfast. I could tell he couldn't say anything because of Sheree, not even about how my hair color was goth black. He wasn't going to defend me. He wasn't going to do anything at all even when it was in front of his face. I knew I had to fend for myself. I put my cereal bowl in the sink, slung my backpack over my shoulder, and walked down the hall to catch a ride with Joann to school. I saw Grandma in her room, eating her tomato and mayo sandwich there instead of by the window. Her eyes welled up.

"I'm so sorry, honey," she said. "I can't say anything, or I'll get into trouble." Then she winced. "If I had known it was going to be like this, I would have left you in Scotland School."

Sheree's anger seemed to frighten Dad and grandmother, and they found themselves walking on eggshells as she raged against one of us or threw everything out of the fridge. Timid Grandma was soft-spoken and kind, and couldn't bear to stand up to Sheree.

But Grandma's sadness began to disappoint me. I always told her I wanted Dad back before I came to live with her full-time. When she picked me up from Scotland School for the summer, I'd pick tomatoes and peas from my part of her garden and chatter about dad.

"Grandma, you're going to send those pictures of me to Dad, right?" I asked.

Back then, she would try to keep her focus on the tomato she plucked from the garden, examining it. "I can't call him," she told me. "I hadn't really talked to him."

The truth was, he didn't want to see me.

Grandma had tried to get the family back together. That's why Dad and Sheree were even in her home in the first place. It had spectacularly backfired.

As I saw the regret on Grandma's face, I thought of my grandfather who had long passed away, who loved me unconditionally. "You're just like your dad," Grandpa said one time. "You're special."

Joann was able to get my hair a little lighter when I went to her house after school. The yellow with the black on top made it look like red highlights. Joann had lightened it up enough to make me feel better, and Sheree didn't even notice because I told her the black color was coming out when I washed it. Then we went for a hike. I didn't have a bike to take me everywhere, so I relied on running the seven miles to Joann's house. Then we'd walk to the gas station for cigarettes a mile and a half down the road. With a cigarette in my mouth, I'd get out my sketchpad and draw the flowers dotting the country scenery.

These afternoons helped me carve out a life beyond Sheree's view. I mowed grass and babysat to make money so I'd never have to ask Sheree to drive me to the store again. Then, Joann would hold onto my money and get me what I needed. Over at her mom's house, she was making her squirrel pot pie, from squirrels Joann's brother had trapped and cleaned. If my mom had seen a squirrel like Chatty being folded into puff pastry, she would have freaked out. While I loved squirrels too, sitting around a loving table with a homemade meal made me feel like part of a family. It made me feel comfortable enough to tell her what was going on at my house.

But it backfired. In the country, it seemed people didn't want to get involved in each other's problems. They were happy to listen, particularly since Grandma was well-known in the community. However, that was where it began and ended.

When I returned home and turned my key in the lock, I saw Sheree in the foyer, her lips pursed. I knew this look from Mom. She was ready to pounce.

"You smell like smoke," she said.

My face turned white.

"Have you been smoking?"

Technically yes, but that was yesterday and I'd taken a shower.

"No, I haven't," I said.

"I know you did." She took a step toward me.

She slapped me hard across the face. I could feel the drops of blood spill from my nose and splatter on the ground. Before I could escape, she grabbed my hair and dragged me around the house. I wailed and screamed for Dad. "You're just like your mother," she said through clenched teeth. "Your mother is nothing, and you're nothing too."

Sheree hurled me into my room and slammed the door. I could hear her stomping away and dialing the kitchen phone. I had no idea who she was talking to, but what she was saying about me made my eyes widen. She could have been talking to a juvenile detention center.

"We need to do something about your daughter," she said.

Oh no, she's talking about me to Mom.

When I heard her slam the phone back onto the receiver, I knew what had to happen next. I couldn't stay here anymore. Grandma couldn't protect me. Dad wouldn't. At 15 years old, I'd endured Sheree's wrath for long enough. I had to get out.

A few days later, locked in my room and looking in my mirror, I winced as I touched the bald spots on my head. Sheree had grabbed my hair so violently—not once, but numerous times, and it was starting to show. I couldn't hide it from anyone, and Joann was already worried. I wasn't going to stick around.

I packed a couple of things in my backpack, and left out of the bedroom window because Sheree was attending another party that night. Walking onto the highway, I tried to remember how to get back to Harrisburg. I'd have to walk twenty miles from Grandma's house. I found myself at Gibson's Rock, a dangerous circular road. There, I stuck out my thumb, ready to hitch a ride.

A tan, beat-up Impala putt-putted down the hill and came to a stop, revealing an older, kind-faced couple who were on their way back to Harrisburg. I sat in between them as we drove to my mom's latest address, not the house on Dunkle Street, but one I'd heard Bernie helped her find. I thanked the couple and walked down the driveway, knocking on the door.

Bernie answered, her eyes wide with surprise. She immediately invited me in. This was not the house on Dunkle Street with the dirty mattresses. Chatty was long gone, having passed away while I was in Scotland School. This was a proper two-story row house typical of Philly and Harrisburg, and Mom was renting out the second floor. I walked into one of the freshly-vacuumed rooms she'd decorated in a Japanese motif, and then into a porch Mom had turned into a screened room. Bernie seemed to be a positive influence in her life. To think that coming to Mom's house was a relief seemed backwards, but with the bald spots on my head aching, I hoped she'd want to keep me this time.

I had spent so much time learning how to not love my mom, because it hurt when I loved her, that I now wondered if it was safe to unlearn it. She came downstairs, looking confused yet happy to see me. Although it still didn't seem natural for her to hug me, she patted my shoulder and told me she'd call Dad so I could bring back the rest of my belongings. Grabbing her shirt, I looked at her intensely and said, "I can't go through this again. Dad doesn't care about me and he only cares about Sheree. Do you promise I can come back?"

"Of course," she said. "We'll just get your clothes."

I believed her. A couple of days later, we got into the car to drive to Grandma's house. As we got closer, though, I started to panic. My body was covered in black and blue marks. My nose ached. The closer we got to the house, the more afraid I became. Something felt wrong here. Were we really just going back to get my clothes?

Sheree opened the front door and sneered, "Hello, Elise." The two women looked like formidable opponents assessing each other, people who deeply disliked the other but seemed to get off on their mutual distaste. My heart started to pound as I walked into the foyer.

As soon as I walked in, I saw Dad, my twin brothers and Grandma all sitting in the kitchen, where Sheree took her place. When I came in with Mom and Bernie, it felt like they were all waiting for me. Except for Grandma, who had a disturbed look on her face, everyone seemed to have been anticipating my arrival. The tension in the room hung like a noose around my neck. It was like entering a ring in hell. You could've beat me all day long and it wouldn't have felt as bad as this did. Sheree glared at Mom. Dad kept his eyes down seemingly in an effort to appease Sheree.

"What's going on?" I asked. "I just need to get my stuff."

"No, you need to sit down," said Sheree.

I looked at Mom and panicked.

"We need you to sit down, Angel," Mom said. Dad nodded.

"We can't handle her," said Sheree, talking about me as if I wasn't there. "I caught her playing with meat and knives."

What?! I thought.

"Well, I can't handle her," Mom said. "She doesn't listen to me either.'

"They should have named you Devil," said Billy. It was clear he was taking his orders from the adults.

I felt like I was floating over my own body. Shutting down, falling apart, and feeling like nothing. I was trying not to listen to what they said.

"This feels like hell and I don't need to stay here," I said, starting to get up from my chair.

"No, you're going to listen," said Dad, pushing my shoulder and forcing me to sit down. "We're the adults. You're going to stay here until we find a place for you to go."

"Like a mental institution," said Sheree. My mom nodded in agreement.

I looked at Grandma. "Say something," I pleaded with her.

She looked down.

"Bernie, you know this isn't true," I said. "Tell them it isn't true."

Bernie looked down too.

It was so surreal; they were talking about someone they didn't even know. I never played with knives. I never played with meat. This wasn't me at all.

Clearly from their discussion, they were planning on putting me away somewhere, and it wouldn't be at home.

I was the one who was black and blue.

I was not going to be blamed for something an adult was doing to me.

Not anymore.

But where would I go?

For three days afterward, Sheree left me in my room. I could only use the bathroom when no one was around. Sheree told me when to leave and when to eat. I had to sneak into the kitchen when my brothers were in school or Sheree was walking down the driveway to get the mail. In the room, lying in bed, I was sobbing. I had no one. Nobody. No place to go.

My spirit began to lift out of my body, swirling and making me feel like I wasn't in bed anymore. It felt like I died. I laid in bed and couldn't move my body. I couldn't scream. I couldn't breathe. My heart was racing. It was like my spirit was trying to leave the house. I felt like I was watching it, but it was energy floating around the room. There had to be an escape from this room, because I wasn't going to make it if I stayed here. No one would, or could, save me. I wasn't going to another school. Rather, I was going to live with my friends, whether it was on the streets or in their homes. I gave no thought to hitchhiking like I had before, since someone might pick me up and bring me right back here.

My only visits were with Grandma, who came into my room and said she was as scared of Sheree as I was. After watching how Sheree could trap me like this in my room, Grandma felt helpless. She said, "I don't feel safe here, and so I'm going to leave." She couldn't take care of herself and me, and so Aunt Lucy picked her up. Aunt Lucy didn't know me that well, and Grandma was too scared to even ask if I could go with her. She didn't want any conflict, just to escape the situation. After she left, this was it for me: she had been my only source of compassion, the only person who talked to me. Now she was gone.

A few hours later, I planned my escape too.

"I'm going to the store," I heard Sheree say to a friend on the phone. Then I heard the front door shut. I ran into the living room and looked out the bay windows. I watched her drive down the acre-long driveway. *Please turn left*, I begged inside, knowing I could walk out and turn right toward where I needed to go. As if willing it to happen, she made a left. All I had to do was make a right.

This was my cue to leave. With a shaky heart but a strong-willed resolve, I grabbed my toothbrush and a few of my things as fast I could. Then I ran into the kitchen to stuff my backpack with cheese crackers, peanut butter, and granola bars—anything that could sustain me. Then I walked out the front door. Shivering in the cold, I walked down the driveway lined with bare trees. I took a deep breath and turned right, ready to make the twenty-mile walk to Harrisburg.

Chapter 5

For three days in a row, I found myself in an alley behind 14th Street in Harrisburg at 3:00 a.m., smoking a cigarette. I was 15 years old, bruised, hopeless, and foggy as to where I would find shelter. Perhaps some divine spirit was watching this scene and saying, "We've seen this movie before." Although it was under different circumstances, Mom had found herself in a similar situation on that Atlantic City pier. It was like we suffered a shared abandonment in parallel universes. We were both fleeing what felt like abuse to us. All of our resources had been taken away. Going outside and staying there seemed to be our only options.

A chill rippled through my sweater. Without a blanket, my cardigan became my only source of warmth. My backpack was my bed, toiletry carrier, and a weapon should I need to defend myself. I smashed my backpack into a pillow-like shape and rested my head. I jumped when I heard rats scuttling around the garbage bins. I choked on the smell of rotting trash, the foulness of old food, and molded cloth. Bums in tattered clothing came in and out of the alley, but I didn't fear them as much as the rats. Although I was scared, I felt safer here than in that house.

The next morning, I looked up to see a man standing over me. I squinted my eyes: it was Michael Good, a friend of Mom's. Michael was thin, in his mid-twenties, with gaunt cheeks. He looked like Jesus with his rough, frizzy hair and spoke with an endearing soft lisp. He was on his way to my mom's house, since it was the alleyway between him and my mom's house. It was as if I was subconsciously waiting for my mom to come get me, and this was the rare instance where it was a welcome relief to see one of her friends come to my rescue.

"What are you doing, Angel?" said Michael. "Bernie's going crazy looking for you, girl. Your mom is worried sick about you too."

Oh sure, I thought. Now my mom wants me to come home. Which home? She'd probably send me back to Sheree's or put me in a mental institution. Going back after running away would mean more yelling, more abuse, more black and blue marks. I could never go back to Grandma's house again. Even my Grandma had fled.

Yet, sleeping on the pavement for the last three nights had left my body feeling like someone had taken a sledgehammer to my lower back and shoulders. A warm bed would be a relief. I mentally sorted through my friends and their parents. I could ask Joann's mom, but I didn't know how long I'd need to stay. I didn't want to be that person who stays too long at someone's house. Looking back up at Michael, I had an idea, although it seemed like a longshot.

"Look, I'll come home if Mom promises not to take me back to Dad's," I said.

"Alright," he said.

"And I want to go to Children and Youth and document what Sheree did to me."

Children and Youth was a local organization that helped kids whose guardians or parents abused them, putting to paper what was secretly happening to them in their homes. This was the only way I would go home, or I'd endure the hardness of the streets.

"Alright," Michael said. "I'll go tell your mom."

While Michael was still convincing me to come back to Mom's house in the alley, Bernie was fuming at Mom. With her arms firmly across her chest, she said, "Elise, you shouldn't have taken her back to Sheree's like that. She can't go there again."

Mom was frantic. "I don't know what we're going to do with her," she said. "I'm sick and the doctor said I can't have any stress."

This "sickness" was something Mom brought up again and again, but we never knew exactly what it was. They wondered where would I go. Scotland School came up again. Or I could be a temporary visitor at their house.

Thelma was home for the weekend from Milton Hershey. She was the only family member *not* there to hear the mental institution talk around the table. She heard Bernie and Mom talking. Thelma shook her head, done with what was going on. She wanted to help me in the capacity she could as a 17-year-old.

Slinging her backpack over her shoulder, Thelma stepped into the kitchen with Bernie and Mom.

"I want Angel to come to Milton Hershey with me," said Thelma.

Mom shook her head. "She'll never get in," she said. "She gets terrible grades in school."

"I'll give her the answers to the test," said Thelma. "You just get her application in and I'll take care of it."

Mom looked at Bernie. There didn't seem to be many options for them or for me. Mom agreed to Thelma's plan. Little did Mom know that Thelma had already gone to her teacher, Mr. Weller, in the admissions building and asked him to consider me as a new student. I had to be accepted into the school before I turned sixteen, so Thelma and I would only have a month to study to get me in by May. I would turn sixteen in June.

Finally, I walked through the door with Michael several hours later. The first thing I saw as I entered the kitchen was Thelma, who always felt like home. Mom glared at me and said, "You should thank your sister. You can stay at school with her, as long as you keep your grades up." I ran into Thelma's arms and hugged her tight. Whether I had last seen her six months or a year before, time and space didn't matter. She was the only one who made me feel truly safe. She was my hero, the person who had saved me from Dunkle Street, Scotland School, and Grandma's house. I hugged her for a long time and she assured me everything was going to be OK from now on. "But we're going to work hard," she assured me, lovingly grabbing my chin and looking into my eyes. "We're going to have to study together."

Thelma was on the student council and one of the mentors in the school. Everyone loved her, so in addition to being my sister and my savior, I had complete faith in her as a school helper. Every weekend, she wrote down the answers so I could memorize them, and whenever I drifted off, she'd stop, look down, grab my chin and say, "Angel, pay attention." Her stern look snapped me back into the moment.

Each day, she drilled the answers to the entrance exam into me. We stayed up late at night and walked to the creek near our house. She told me a story to go with the exam question so I could visualize it, and then I would understand. At the water, she started giving me a math problem: "I'm going to take two cups out," she said, holding actual cups in her hands that she swiped from the kitchen. "Then, I'm going to pour two cups out. If I have four cups, two cups are a quarter, a half, or a whole?"

I began visualizing the problem instead of seeing it as writing or I'd write the answers on my hand. "Half?" I asked. Thelma jumped up and down, hugging me.

"You got it, Angel!"

A few weeks later, I sat down, alone, in the empty classroom, where the teacher read the test questions and possible answers to me. Mr. Weller presided over the psychologist proctoring the exam. I kept twirling my hair with my brush, holding it like my lifeline. "Angel, I have to take this while you're taking the test. Don't worry, I'll give it back." I handed the hairbrush to him, reluctantly.

It took two and half hours for me to complete a one-hour test, and Mr. Weller said he'd call my house with my results. I was going to Harrisburg schools in the meantime. When I went home, I willed the phone to ring. Then, the ring came, and Bernie took the call. After listening for a minute, she looked over at Thelma, nodding and smiling.

"They got her in," said Thelma. "They're going to take her at the end of the school year."

I got in one month shy of my sixteenth birthday.

I just made it.

Oh, Bernie and I reported Sheree to Children and Youth. They never pursued any action against Sheree, but at the very least I would never have to live with her again.

It all seemed to be working out. But as my life became more normal, the weight of what happened at Grandma's house still clung to me. The whole scenario of me being the devil hit me. *Wow, was there really something wrong with me? Maybe they named me Angel for a reason.* Maybe I would fail Thelma after all the help she'd given me. I didn't feel worthy of being in this school. Perhaps they would kick me out when they found out I was a fraud.

I didn't want to embarrass Thelma or reveal how much I was struggling in my classes. Then, all the people who loved her would see her little sister couldn't keep up.

There had been so much food at Scotland School, a welcome change from my mom's empty cupboards. When I lived with Sheree, Dad, and Grandma, Sheree had no problem telling me I gained a lot of weight, although at my age it was natural to do so. When I got to 135 pounds, she started saying I was going to get fat like my mom.

Milton Hershey was a lot like Scotland School food-wise, and without Sheree there to scold me, the empty feeling in my stomach was ready for more than the roll, macaroni and cheese, and chicken served at lunch. I couldn't seem to get full when I was eating lunch. *Eat faster*, I told myself, filling myself up faster and faster. One day, I had to run to the bathroom and throw up.

Looking into the toilet, I thought *wow, there was something to this eating-more-and-not -gaining-weight thing.* I felt a wave of euphoria, a sense of satisfaction I could get myself full and not gain weight. Every day after lunch, I'd go into that bathroom, put my fingers down my throat, and let the contents of my lunch rush into the bowl.

At least I could look good at school. As I walked down the hallway from the bathroom, a balding man in a tweed jacket passed by and gave me a small smile and wave.

Thelma saw I was starting to fail school after only a few months. She wanted to help me succeed.

"I need to introduce you to somebody," she said. "His name is Mr. Stacks, the art teacher here." I knew there was no other place for me and I didn't want to get kicked out of school. I couldn't even visualize my future, but I didn't want to fail my sister. I needed to meet Mr. Stacks.

The next day, Thelma introduced me to Mr. Stacks and I recognized him from the hallway greeting of months earlier. I was so scared and yet so excited to meet him. Maybe *he* would understand me. Maybe *he* would be able to help. Super tall, he had beak-like lips and a pear-shape body. He always wore a hat and sweater and looked like a cartoon character from the sixties and seventies. I was mesmerized by the fuzzy hair that grew from his ears. As he looked up from his work, using an airbrush on a sign, I could see he was left-handed like me.

"Hello, Angel," he said. "Take a look around!"

His studio was like an eccentric little village: pottery in one room, paints in the other. He was also a professional sign painter, so there were compressors with the airbrushes all sitting in a neat lineup against the wall. The school let him keep the space for his studio. As soon as I opened the cold metal doors, I felt like I was walking into a new world. Each room of the studio was decorated like the entrance into a business. The hallway to each room was like a street. Some entrances had wooden shingles above the door to represent a roof.

The smell of shellac would become a familiar, welcoming scent, as would the old paint in the studio. In the storage room, there was a recliner, so if I wanted to rest, turn the lights off, or dream, I could. Anytime. I felt like I was in heaven. I'd found my own little paradise. By staying in his class and working on my printing and airbrushing skills, I could skip English and math.

"Anything you want to do," he said. "You can do."

Then Mr. Stacks showed me the airbrush he had been working with. He showed me how to lay a rainbow pattern on the back of a sign. It was a basketball sign, and it had a hand-painted "Go Spartans" on the back. Together, we made a misty background on it. When I was in this studio, in this safe place of endless creation and creativity, I could use anything I wanted. I wanted to make a painting on my own.

When I made art, I felt free of all the pain in my life. But that airbrush was another level. I wanted to have it so I could make things, and then make money. Since I feared never being able to make art here and being moved again, I wanted to take the airbrush for myself. Just in case I had to leave this place, I'd still have something I could use to make money.

I slipped the airbrush into my pocket.

A few days later, Mr. Stacks looked all over his studio for that airbrush, and of course I knew exactly where it was: it was safe and sound in my backpack. Doing this to my new friend seemed cruel. My heart sank as he looked around for it. He was someone who genuinely didn't want anything from me, but I had stolen something he loved.

"Did you take the airbrush?" he asked, his voice steady, without the usual explosive anger I had come to expect from adults who accused me of stealing or otherwise doing something I wasn't supposed to. I shook my head "no."

"Well, I guess, someone else must have needed it more than me," he said with a shrug, and started to clean a corner of the studio. *Mr. Stacks must be OK.*

"Someone else must have needed it more than me," he repeated.

I felt a sick drop in my stomach. Mr. Stacks seemed to be a kind person, and here I was stealing his airbrush. How could I hurt this man after all he was doing for me? I needed to put it back, fast. Unlike the time I stole Mom's food stamps, I regretted what I'd done.

When he was looking in another part of the room, I placed it in the storage room.

"I found it, Mr. Stacks," I said. He smiled.

The incident was never mentioned again. I vowed to never steal again after that.

Mr. Stacks and I had a daily routine. After the homeroom bell rang, I was allowed to go downstairs to his studio and we'd create art. He asked me to read something in the studio one day, and I couldn't read it. He could see that I could only read on a third-grade reading level. As someone who was in charge of special needs kids, he wanted to help me. From that point on he taught me how to read, one letter at a time. He color-coordinated the letters, highlighting the parts that were initially hard for me to understand. Never once did he let me give up on a word or a sentence. Knowing I was dyslexic, he'd go one letter at a time. This helped me with my spelling, as well as making our airbrushed signs. Then we'd go to Denny's for brunch. While we ate, he'd encourage me to talk and tell more stories by asking, "What else?" Afterwards, he drove me to K-Mart to buy whatever I needed: shampoo, conditioner, clothes, and makeup.

At the beginning of each day, he'd sit there with his beak of a mouth, his top lip moving around as he worked with me on each part of the words, sentences and paragraphs.

"OK, let's sound it out together," he said, highlighting the letters I switched around. His plan was for me to keep excelling in the printer shop, and allow me to graduate with a printing curriculum. I learned how to paint murals and signs as a potential career. I entered sign-making contests at school. I even won third place. I won an actual contest thanks to him.

Then some evenings, he'd have me over to his house for dinner. His wife would make pot roast, mashed potatoes, and peas. I looked at them and thought this would be the ideal life. I could get used to feeling like a part of their family. I wanted to live here.

"Pops, can I live with you?" I said, calling him by my nickname for him.

He smiled. "I wish you could." He and his wife shared a knowing look filled with something I didn't understand, because as much as I seemed to be part of the fabric of Mr. Stacks' everyday life, parts of his day were still concealed from me.

At another dinner about a year later, I expected it would be the three of us, but it was us and another couple, who smiled wanly at me at the table. I moved my peas and potatoes around, unsure why Mr. Stacks was introducing me to these new people. The conversation turned to homes, and the guy in the couple said, "We have a great big backyard, Angel. You will love it."

I will love it? Will means the future, that I *will* be where you're saying and that I will love it. It seemed that Mr. Stacks was trying to match me up with this couple who could visit me at school and be like him and Mrs. Stacks. There was no way I was going to leave Pops, so was he trying to get rid of me? A rush of anxiety washed over me. This had all been too good to be true, and it was time for me to be shown the door, as usual. I was going to be cast out for reasons unknown to me. Or perhaps all that we'd done together—sign-making, winning contests, creating art—didn't mean anything. Maybe it had all been busywork.

"Pops, I just want to be with you," I said, slamming my napkin down and leaving the table. His wife ran after me and gently took my hand in hers.

"Sweetie, don't be mad at him," she said.

"Why not?" I asked. "He doesn't want me; you don't really want me. You're trying to get me to go off with these people I don't even know."

"Calm down. Pops loves you and wants to be sure you're with people who love you too."

"He's trying to get rid of me," I said.

The lines on her face deepened. "He just wants to be sure you're safe," she said.

The next day, I sat under the bleachers to smoke a cigarette. I ran track as part of P.E. Thinking about how Mr. Stacks must not have wanted me to live with him, or how I really meant anything to him, I needed to blow off my studio time. As I took a long drag, a dark-haired student sat next to me. His sister and I shared space at the student home, and I'd seen him around. His eyes sparkled.

"May I?" he asked as he looked at my cigarette. I let him take a long drag before I put it back to my lips. There was something about him that was dangerous in a wholesome way. I could pretend to get into danger with him, more mischief than actual, full-on troublemaking.

"The name's EJ," he said.

"Angel," I replied. It was clear I needed to make more friends—allies who would be around me when I graduated, especially since Mr. Stacks clearly didn't want me around forever. And the way EJ was looking at me right now? Perhaps he would be more than a friend.

EJ and I began spending all of our time together. We'd meet up under the bleachers and talk about everything. I really felt like he was listening to me when I talked about my past. We passed a cigarette in between each other, taking long drags. I could look into his eyes for long stretches of time, something that was rare for me since I always felt easily distracted.

One late afternoon as we watched a football practice from our perch, our fingers grazed each other. I looked down, feeling my stomach flip. I wasn't sure if it was a good or bad flip.

Two years later, I graduated from high school. EJ and I were an on-again, off-again couple, although EJ wanted to be more on as much as I was off. He bought me flowers and was still the most attentive listener I'd ever known. I just never knew how to feel about him.

In the meantime, my post-high school job projects were looking good. Mr. Stacks got me into an apprentice program at Stiegel Printing, a printing company in Lancaster, Pennsylvania, and found a permanent home for me with Mr. Sanko, one of the other teachers and a good friend of his. On graduation day, he handed me a bank statement showing he'd been putting away the money I earned at my cashier job at McDonald's and airbrushing t-shirts in the park.

"I'll get you a check from that bank account soon," he said. I looked at the account balance statement in the room where we had spent many hours working together, him building me a backup from the foundation. If I had been more in tune with my emotions, I would've cried, but instead, I said, "You made me, Mr. Stacks."

He smiled and nodded. "You made yourself, Angel."

This was the man who listened to me like no one else. For these two years, he very rarely left the basement, but he would look for me in classrooms if I missed coming into the studio. If he scolded, he used a stern voice, but never yelled. Whenever he was upset, it was his disappointment that hurt my heart. Feeling a pang of guilt, I should have known he was always there for me, even if for some reason he wouldn't let me stay with him.

On graduation night, EJ and I were free from school and ready to celebrate. That June evening, we took a joyride in his deep green, four-seater low-rider that bounced up in the air with the shocks. The air wafted through my hair, sending it all over the place. We talked about the future as we drove down to his mom's house in Philadelphia. Looking at his dreamy eyes so focused on the road ahead, I began to see EJ in a new light. He was someone who could look after me since Mr. Stacks wasn't there to ensure I was doing well every day. I was starting a whole new life, and at least I could take part of my high school days with me. I still had questions about the future, ones that could be made less scary to answer with EJ at my side: *when would I move in with Mr. Stacks' friend, Mr. Sanko? What would life be like without seeing Mr. Stacks every day?*

At EJ's mom's house, he received "Happy Graduation" cards stuffed with cash, which made us both giddy. Then his mom gave me a hug and headed upstairs to bed. We went up soon after, where EJ showed me his room. It had a bed full of stuffed animals.

"Wow, this is really cool," I said, sitting on the bed and giving a small bounce. Then I looked up at EJ, who was giving me the same smoldering look he did under the bleachers the day we met. I'd never found myself in a situation where I welcomed such a stare. It sent a vibration down my arms and legs. As he unbuttoned his shirt, I waited for him to envelope me with his body, to be taken away, to feel a sense of romance pouring over me. Or at least what I had thought was romance. We kissed and fell into the bed, taking off each other's clothes, and delving into each other's bodies. Although we were technically having sex, it was more like two kids playing house, a fun activity, not some steamy affair. At least for me.

A few weeks later, I was airbrushing a sign at the printing company when I felt bile rising in my throat. I quickly dropped the airbrush and ran into the bathroom. I barely made it before throwing up my breakfast. This wasn't on purpose or an attempt to keep my weight down. I'd gotten past that, thanks to Mr. Stacks. But I felt queasy, and my breasts were tender to the touch as I rubbed my chest to ease it from what I thought was heartburn.

What's wrong with me? I thought.

Chapter 6

When I got home from work, EJ had yellow roses in his hand. He'd driven from Philadelphia, as he did every weekend, to come see me. But today he saw me coming in flustered, unable to form sentences and racing around my room. "Slow down, Angel," he said. "Everything's going to be fine. Just tell me what's wrong."

"I don't know what's going on," I said. I described my symptoms: breasts swelling, tender nipples, throwing up at work. My whole body was swollen and all I wanted to do was sleep. "I haven't had my period in almost two months."

EJ studied my face. From his expression, I could see he thought the answer was obvious, but it certainly wasn't clear to me. "Maybe you're pregnant," he said.

"No, no, that can't be it," I said. "Maybe I have a disease." The spread of HIV/AIDS had started since graduation. At the time, no one knew what was causing healthy-looking people to suddenly get sick or die within weeks. Perhaps that was me.

"Maybe you're sick too?" I asked.

EJ didn't look ill at all. Wouldn't he look gaunt or pale or have those lesions? Perhaps his sickness wasn't showing yet. There was no way I was pregnant. We'd only done it on graduation night. Well, maybe a few times since graduation.

"No, I'm not sick," said EJ. "Maybe we should get a pregnancy test for you."

"I'm fine," I said, taking the flowers out of his hand and smelling them. "Let's go to the movies."

But a few days later on my break at work, I started to eliminate factors about why I was feeling how I was. I couldn't get an AIDS test. Maybe I should get a pregnancy test from the drug store, and so I did. I peed on the stick in the company restroom and waited five minutes for the result. Positive meant I was pregnant—negative, not pregnant. Within that time, it came back positive.

I was pregnant.

Sitting on the toilet with my white underwear wrapped around my ankles, every cell in my body jumped then froze. *Maybe the test was wrong*? The packaging crinkled in my hand as I ripped open the second test. Five minutes went by. Positive. Double positive. *I was really pregnant.*

I caught my own horrified expression in the mirror: I was going to be a mom. New life was growing inside of me. A part of me said to be scared about that. How was I going to raise a child when it was hard enough to get myself to work and maintain a life? How could someone whose own mother never acted like a real mom do this?

I flushed the toilet and walked outside, closing the door behind me. The only way to call EJ was Mr. Sanko's company phone, so I waited until he looked engrossed in his accounting figures on paper. When I dialed EJ, he picked up almost immediately. I told him I had taken two pregnancy tests and they both came back positive.

"What are we going to do if this is real?" I asked, twirling my hair. Of course, it was real, but it still didn't seem like it. I still doubted whether I was actually sick or perhaps it was all in my head. There I was, a graduate of high school with a great job at a printing company—with a baby on the way. My one shot at a better life for myself seemed to be slipping away.

"I'll take care of you," EJ said in a tender voice. "You can move out of Mr. Sanko's and we'll get a place of our own. I love you, Angel. Nothing's gonna change that."

EJ's words and I love you's passed through me, never seeming to linger in my heart. Although we had spent so much time together and shared beautiful conversations, he was still more of a friend than a romantic interest in my mind. My mind knew I should say "I love you" back. Sure, I was prepared to possibly have HIV/AIDS and face imminent death, but I wasn't ready to have a child with someone I couldn't say I love you to.

How would I tell Mr. Stacks? His words about EJ began to play in my head like one of Thelma's tapes to me at Scotland School. Mr. Stacks didn't seem to like where EJ and I were headed. During our breakfasts at Denny's, he'd say to me, "Don't mess around with guys. Once you get yourself a job and savings, you can start dating. You've had enough hard times. I want you to stay focused with Mr. Sanko. Stay there and keep working."

As I held the phone to my ear listening to EJ make plans, I kept visualizing Mr. Stacks digging into his scrambled eggs as he told me to focus on my career. The memory of him caring so much about me versus EJ doing the same thing in the current time couldn't compare. Tears rolled down my face as I thought about how much I'd disappointed Pops.

Several hours later, I clocked out and arrived at Mr. Sanko's house to find EJ with a stuffed teddy bear. Was this the time to tell him I didn't really like babies? That I thought they were icky because they slobbered, threw up, and couldn't control their own bodily functions? The actual caring for a baby seemed gross to me.

Or maybe my old friend, God, knew something I didn't: this baby was no accident. Maybe he felt this is what I needed. I had been looking for someone who would love me forever since I was a kid. I put my hand on my stomach. *Oh, God,* I thought, *if you think I'll be a good mother, please allow this child to love me and I will love this child back so, so much.*

God must trust me to be a responsible mom. Why couldn't I trust myself?

A few afternoons after taking that pregnancy test, I went to Thelma's place, which she was renting from Mom and Bernie. Telling Mr. Stacks would have to wait, especially since I was gold in his eyes. I wasn't ready to tarnish that. I still wasn't sure if the test was real, and maybe if it wasn't real, I wouldn't want to upset him. I would have to deal with him asking "Why are you having a child right now?"

With those two words—"I'm pregnant"—Thelma leaned back in her chair, then forward to look into my eyes. She was mining my face to see if I fully understood what was going on. She knew I had a harder time learning in school, and that carried over into understanding sexuality. I twirled my hair, uncomfortable, waiting for her to say something.

"Who's the father?" she asked.

"EJ," I said.

"When did this happen?"

"Graduation night, I think. We haven't done it since. Well, not often anyway."

"What about birth control? Did either of you think about that?"

I shrugged, which made Thelma sigh. We both weren't taught much about sex and sexuality as kids and young adults. After a few beats, Thelma seemed to be collecting herself for what she would say next.

"Angel," she said, "You promised you weren't going to do this to another kid and have them go through what we did."

I took a deep breath before answering her. "I need someone to love me back," I said. "I need something to love that nobody can take from me."

Thelma nodded, her eyes beginning to glisten with tears. She reached out to take my hand. "I'm going to help you through this," she said. "First, we need to go to the doctor."

I had to go live with Thelma. Since she was living with Bernie and Mom, she would need to tell them the news. While Mom and I had a difficult relationship, I still wanted her to be happy I was pregnant, and that she was becoming a grandma. For the most part, she was pleasant about it, but not overly effusive. Then, all of us made an action plan: I would sign up to receive public assistance and doctor's wellness visits from Hamilton House Center, an affordable healthcare clinic for those who couldn't otherwise afford it. EJ would move to Harrisburg and rent an apartment for us three. After making these plans, I walked into the printing company and told Mr. Sanko I couldn't work there anymore. I needed a less demanding job where I could make money and stay healthy while I was pregnant. He didn't seem to care either way, although he said, "You might want to tell Mr. Stacks."

I walked into Denny's wearing a baggy shirt and jeans. Pops was sitting in our usual spot with the newspaper concealing his face. I could see his hat and sweater peeking from the sports section as I sat down beside him. He then revealed his face, and my heart sank; not only was he smiling so big, but his mouth seemed to take up more of his face than usual. His cheeks were sunken in and his skin was pale, and his usual smattering of ear hair was out of control.

"Pops, are you ok?" I asked, trying not to sound stunned. "You're losing a lot of weight."

"Oh, I'm fine," he said, waving his hand. "Let's talk about you, Angel. I hear you have something to tell me?"

I'd told him on the phone this wasn't a usual visit, and that we needed to talk in person.

"Well, it's not easy to tell you this," I said. "But I'm pregnant."

The server brought over two steaming plates of scrambled eggs, bacon, and hash browns as if on cue. We watched him put down the plates, which felt like it was happening in slow motion. As soon as he left, Mr. Stacks picked up his fork and began rummaging through his eggs. He kept staring at his eggs as he moved them around with his fork, and then cut into a hash brown without eating it. He seemed to be searching for the right response on his plate, but it wasn't coming.

"Alright, Angel, what are we going to do?" he finally said.

"Well, I was hoping you might know," I replied. "EJ is getting us a house here and Thelma is going to help me go to the doctor. But I need a new job."

Mr. Stacks nodded, reading between the lines that EJ was the father of my baby. "That's important," he said. "You still need to earn a living. I don't want you to have to depend on EJ for every penny. Remember it's always best to have your own money and resources."

He finally took a bite of his eggs, but the piece was so small. I'd never seen him eat like this, moving the food around on his plate and eating so little of it. As he chewed, he suddenly started coughing louder and louder. He had to grab a napkin and cover his mouth until it subsided.

"Are you sure you're alright, Pops?" I asked, furrowing my eyebrows.

"I'm fine," he said. "An egg just went down the wrong pipe. Now, let's focus on you."

Mr. Stacks helped me fill out public assistance paperwork. He got me some art jobs painting signs on the side that would give me an income. The money was cash only, so I could keep the full amount. Then, Bernie helped me get a job as a cashier at a penny store, since she was friends with the Solomon family. They also ran the candy store outside of the school where I had led that sugar-fueled mutiny years ago.

When I wasn't miscounting change, Mr. Stacks would find me small mural jobs so I could keep up with the trade he'd set me up for in school. Each time I saw him, he looked a little thinner. I wanted to see him more often, to restart our everyday Denny's breakfasts instead of having them only once and awhile, but he said it was best to keep it once a week. "I don't want to tire you out," he'd say. "Besides, you have a baby to love coming."

I visited the house to see Bernie and Thelma because they told me I needed to watch something special on TV with them. The space shuttle Challenger was about to launch into space with two female astronauts among the all-male crew: Christa McAuliffe and Judith Resnik. History was being made today, Thelma kept telling me, and it would be good for my future baby and me to see this. Christa was the astronaut who seemed to interest me the most. She was a teacher in New Hampshire whom NASA had selected for their "Teacher in Space" program. I smiled, thinking about how adorable Mr. Stacks would look in an astronaut uniform being blasted into space.

As we watched the launch live in the backroom of the house, everyone got quiet as the shuttle rocketed into the sky. Then, seventy-five seconds later, the capsule became engulfed in black and white smoke and fire, and blew apart. Something went wrong, and we didn't know what it was. My stomach tightened. As soon as that happened, my baby started turning around, reacting to my emotions. I held my belly. *We're ok*, I tried to tell her. Not only was I feeling confusion and sadness, but she was too.

Breaking news took a closer look at what happened: the space shuttle Challenger had exploded, instantly killing everyone onboard. Including Christa. The Teacher in Space. The teacher that could have been Mr. Stacks taking one small step for man, one giant leap for mankind. But they hadn't even left the atmosphere.

I was in labor for three days. Early in the morning almost three months after the Challenger exploded, I was admitted to the hospital. I was given a paper gown and socks and placed in a sterile white bed with cold metal railings. The room reeked of antiseptic and iodine. Fluorescent lights blasted my face and gave me a headache. I was sweating as the doctors barked at me, trying to get me to focus. *Focus, Angel.*

I was on medication for eighteen hours to induce labor. The doctors even had to break my water, and it was getting so bad that the baby was distressed. If the baby didn't come in an hour or two after this, they would have to do a c-section. Thelma held my hand as I screamed.

"I don't know if I can do this," I said, my forehead dripping and my face turning red.

"You can do it," she kept saying, never doubting that I could.

Finally, I gave a few final pushes, and the baby was out of me. The sounds of crying filled the small room as the doctor raised the baby up and placed her in my arms: a daughter. Looking into her face with her small nose and mouth that opened wide with screams, I felt the same as I did when I watched the Challenger explosion: I could sense her feelings, I could feel her in my arms as I had felt her in utero, but numbness dulled my insides. The only physical reaction I could truly pinpoint was how cold I felt after feeling hot during labor. No matter how many blankets Thelma brought over to me, I was still shivering.

I would name her Shaena Bernice, after Bernie, who had always been kind despite how my mom treated me. I had a big sense of relief that she had come out healthy, and then they took her away and cleaned her up. I sensed there was a way I was supposed to feel, but I had no idea how to access it. I was more emotional because it was over and there was a reward of a baby. EJ stood by me, kissed me on the forehead and said I'd "done great."

The machines whirled in my recovery room. The sounds of the metal wheels on the floor screeched when the bed moved. I'd been placed in a room with a little curtain between two people. The doctors were kind, yet matter-of-fact, coming in to teach me how to change the baby and breastfeed, which only lasted a day because it felt awkward to me. I was afraid I'd crush this little baby in my arms. I feared I'd hold her too tight or not tight enough.

She had two huge dimples on her cheeks, so big and dented in I thought something was wrong with her. "What is that?" I asked the doctor. "Is that normal?"

Apparently, it was.

I tried holding her close to my chest, trying to see if it would trigger any emotion in me. *How do I take care of this thing?* I wondered. I was afraid I was going to break her. I kept her bassinet by my bed. I kept poking her, fearing she wouldn't wake up. I couldn't get to the emotion of love, and I didn't want to tell anyone because I didn't really trust anyone. I thought they were going to take her from me, and my mom was always telling people I wasn't going to be a good mother.

Just then, Mom and Thelma came into my room. Thelma had a look on her face that said she'd been trying to wrangle Mom into behaving like a normal new grandma: excited, happy, and supportive. Mom tried to pretend I hadn't heard her behind the curtain saying, "How is Angel going to do this?" to Thelma, who assured her I would be a great mom.

One person was missing: Mr. Stacks.

Shaena kept screaming. In the middle of the night, EJ and I both got up to take care of her, although he was better at making her comfortable. She would fall asleep in his arms. When I held her, she screamed harder. If I was awake by myself, I felt hopeless. And to make it worse, Mom was suddenly taking over.

"Bring her here," Mom said. "I'll take her."

I didn't want to ask my mom for help, for her to know why I was feeling this way. Bernie could rock Shaena and she would fall asleep. I wanted to learn how to do that, but no one was teaching me what to do. They just wanted me to bring her over. Shaena would just start cooing in Bernie's arms, and while I wanted her to be happy, I knew I wanted to figure this out for myself.

After calling her every day since Shaena's birth, Mrs. Stacks finally scheduled a meeting with Mr. Stacks and me. He had to meet the baby, but it wasn't just a social moment for me: I needed to know I could take care of her. The hospital couldn't prepare me for that. Even Thelma could only go so far. As soon as I saw him with his paper over his face at our usual booth at Denny's, a sense of relief came over me. I sat down next to him and he finally saw my daughter. His eyes seemed bigger since his face was so much thinner, but the delight they carried seemed to light up his whole body.

"Why, hello there," he said as I handed him Shaena. "Look at you!"

She cooed in his arms and looked at him as he rocked her. Of course, she loved him like I did.

"I'm afraid Mom is going to take her from me," I said.

He looked at me, curious. "Why, Angel?"

I paused, feeling tears start to form in my eyes. "Because I'm having a hard time feeling love for her," I said.

"What do you mean?" he asked.

"Well, I feel responsible for her, but then I get upset when she screams. Sometimes I have to put her in another room and hold my ears."

Mr. Stacks hugged Shaena. He looked deeply at my face, seeming to have the right words but was searching for the right way to say them.

"Do you feel love for me?" he asked.

"Of course, I do," I replied.

He gave Shaena a little hug. "See, I love you, and I love this baby," he said, and then slowly handed her to me. "You can love this little baby. Here, try it."

I held Shaena as he said, "You love this baby," and then he took her back into his arms, my hands and his hands intertwined around this little girl. We were all connected to each other. That's when I started to cry as he placed her in my arms again. For the first time, she didn't just feel like a small meatloaf: she was starting to feel like my daughter.

"Do you feel that?" he asked, looking at her and then back at me.

I nodded, tears splashing on Shaena's receiving blanket.

"This is love," said Mr. Stacks. "You do love her, honey."

Finally, I felt it, watching Shaena'd laugh reveal her dimples. Tears streamed down my face. I had this breakthrough: I was going to be her mom for life. I was never going to stop learning how to love her, because Mr. Stacks knew I could do that. I looked into his eyes, which appeared more sunken than I'd ever seen them. His face was so thin, I kept thinking as he and I passed Shaena between each other, the three of us enjoying a Grand Slam breakfast and learning how to love. *He can't be sick.*

"What's the matter, Pops?" I finally asked.

"Oh, nothing, I've just been losing weight. What, I don't look good?"

"Seriously, are you ok? Do you promise me you're ok?"

"Yes, I'm good."

I still felt in my soul something was wrong with Pops, but I didn't want to lose him. Asking him how he was feeling and potentially finding out the answer seemed devastating. I couldn't raise my baby without Mr. Stacks. A world without him wasn't possible. Mr. Stacks had empowered me to find the answer about being a good mom. "God is in you," he said, patting my shoulder. "If you can't figure it out, you need to learn. I'm not always going to be here."

You gotta let him rest, Angel, was what Mrs. Stacks kept telling me when I called to ask if Pops could come with Shaena and me to breakfast at Denny's each week. It had been several weeks since our last meal there. Now I knew something was wrong. I bundled up Shaena and we drove to Milton Hershey School. I was going to track down Pops in his old studio and find out what was really going on. He wasn't there. I raced through the once familiar halls with Shaena bouncing in my arms, setting my sights on Mrs. Stacks' office. She also worked alongside Pops, and I'd found myself in her office a few times, including today.

"You have to tell me what's going on with Pops," I demanded. "Something is wrong."

"Ok, honey," she said, sighing. "Let me tell you."

Pops was really sick, and had been for a long time. During our family dinners, the time he invited that one couple over, the times at Denny's when he wouldn't eat his eggs. He'd been diagnosed with prostate cancer. He was going through chemo in Philadelphia once a week. Stunned, I started to feel dizzy. *This couldn't be happening.* I never knew Mr. Stacks was spending parts of his day sitting in a hospital gown on a cushy patient chair talking to an oncologist. I didn't know he would nod and pretend to understand what his doctor was telling him. I didn't know he had cancer and no one knew what had caused it, maybe the paint fumes from the studio. I didn't know that the cancer was quietly growing inside of Mr. Stacks each time we sounded out a word together, ate scrambled eggs at Denny's, and bought shampoo at K-Mart.

I put my hand over my mouth.

"No, this can't be real," I said.

"I'm sorry, sweetie, but it is," she said. "We have the best doctors working to make Pops all better. There's nothing for you to worry about."

All of the energy left my body. I barely had enough energy in my voice to say "no" or form any other words. My voice was gone. Mrs. Stacks' eyes filled with tears, and she melted in my arms when she reached out to me and cried with me in the studio where Mr. Stacks and I had spent so many hours working on our art. She was trying her best to hold herself together.

"Sweetheart, I have to go back to work," she said.

One year later, Shaena and I visited Mr. Stacks in the hospital. I painted pictures of him, Shaena, and me holding hands. Us in a portrait. I didn't even do that with EJ. I sat next to Mr. Stacks amid the whirl of machines. He was frail, beyond thin. His nose looked huge compared to his face, and his body was disappearing. I'd talk about what we were going to do together. I was determined he would keep getting better. No matter how much I talked with him, he was too weak to form words. He could nod or smile.

"I need you here," I whispered. "Shaena needs you here."

Mr. Stacks looked at me and smiled, weaker than I'd ever seen him. He reached out his hand and put it over mine and Shaena's. I was only 19 years old, Shaena—barely a year old. We needed him to stay. I told him this every time I went to the hospital, which was every single day. The next week, I stopped going to the hospital because I couldn't accept that he was going to die. A few days later, Mrs. Stacks called me. Pops had passed away that night. Inside of me, I kind of already knew he wasn't here anymore, but I remember holding Shaena so tightly. "Thank you for teaching me how to love her," I thought about Mr. Stacks. "And you'll be with me forever. Every time I look at her. Every time I feel love. I am going to make you so proud of me. I'm going to be the best person in the world and show everyone that you did good."

I was going to be the best mom.

You're going to see me every day, Pops.

You're going to see I was worth it.

That it was worth loving me like you did.

Chapter 7

After Mr. Stacks passed, I hoarded memories of him—things that would help me continue to blossom. Things that would help me grow into the person he hoped I'd be back when I first entered his studio. When Shaena was asleep, I rummaged through stacks of cassette tapes he'd given me over the years. Although I listened to some of the tapes he brought me, this pile had gone completely unheard.

One book on tape stuck out to me in particular: *Healing the Child Within: Discovery and Recovery for Adult Children of Dysfunctional Families*. I decided to pop it into my car cassette player and listen to it on the way to and from work at an ad agency, where I painted signs and sold specialties.

My days ran together: I'd drop off Shaena with Mom and Bernie, and allow myself to be taken away into self-discovery. Listening to books rather than struggling to read them on paper made the experience enjoyable, educational, and further imprinted my goal: to make Mr. Stacks proud, always.

Healing the Child Within became one of my major life changers. When I'd go pick up Shaena from Bernie and Mom's, I'd feel like I was bubbling with new ideas. As I put Shaena in her carseat, I'd tell her what I was learning even though I knew an almost two-year-old was more interested in naps and playtime than spiritual growth. Just saying what I learned aloud felt good.

Then I moved on to *Loving Each Other: The Challenge of Human Relationships* by Leo F. Buscaglia, Ph.D. Then books on parenting. I kept listening to these books on tape and I started to feel proud of who I was. I began to make new goals for myself. With my experience in airbrushing and making signs, I could start my own ad agency. To do that though, I would need money to rent office space and equipment.

To raise money, EJ got me a job as a muralist at the pizza joint where he was a driver. I started painting a mural on an under-twenty-one club called the Kauna Club. I was putting everything into it. It was called Kauna because it showed three stories of the ocean. All four walls were covered in the ocean and palm trees, leftover imagery from when I used to airbrush t-shirts in the park. I danced while painting, turning this space with a DJ stand into an oasis. I used the money I made to start my ad agency.

A young, scraggly-haired woman with sunken cheeks came out of the massage parlor next door and stared at my creation. She looked at me and then back at the painting, her expression stoic and unreadable. Then she said, "Nice." That was it. *Nice.*

I nodded and tried to be polite, although I was annoyed.

By the time I got home that night from work, I found EJ passed out on the couch. He was either sleeping or still out delivering pizzas, taking extra shifts so we could make extra money. I put down my purse and sat next to him, admiring his dark, curly hair and shaggy eyebrows framing his closed eyes. Part of me wanted to wake him up so we could talk, since we hadn't talked all day. But I also had to get ready for another full day tomorrow, which meant washing my and Shaena's clothes, tidying up the kitchen, and doing chores until I passed out.

When I wasn't preparing for the next day, I began working my second shift at home: I'd paint in the basement for other freelance art jobs, sometimes until 3:00 a.m. Sometimes, I'd work until the sun came up, and still have to go to work in the morning.

The next night, I arrived home on time and EJ was sitting on the couch eating dinner. He looked up at me walking in. "There's more chili on the stove," he said. "Why don't you come over here and we'll catch up on TV together."

"I'd love to, but I gotta read," I said. Every night when I got home, I'd read the Bible. Although it wasn't a book on tape, I enjoyed taking my time with it, digesting the characters, stories, and truths within its pages. This, along with the books on tape, was making me a better person. A better mom. I was all about making Mr. Stacks proud. EJ and I never seemed to be awake at the same time anymore, let alone present in the same room.

When EJ started coming home later and later, I didn't immediately notice. Most people would have seen their partner wasn't there or at least would have made more of an effort to find out what was going on. I was consumed by listening to tapes, painting at work, or spending time with Shaena that life became one big blur to me. After work one evening, I put my purse down as usual and didn't see EJ sleeping on the couch. He wasn't in the kitchen either, and the sink and countertop were spotless. He hadn't eaten dinner. He probably hadn't come home at all.

Maybe he got into a car accident, I thought. Perhaps he was making a pizza delivery and hit a tree or someone hit him on the road. I dialed the pizza joint.

"Hello?" a deep voice said on the other line.

"Hey, EJ?" I asked. There was a different tone in his voice.

"No, it's Harry," the voice said. "Are you looking for EJ?"

"Well, yes, that's why I called."

"I think he's working on a car," he said. "He'll probably be done soon."

"Oh, alright. Please tell him Angel called."

"Yeah, sure thing, Angel."

I decided to surprise EJ at work. He was probably almost done fixing that car and we could meet up. I put on a little blush and lipstick before heading out, putting Shaena in her car seat and taking a late drive to the pizza joint. I wanted to be spontaneous, to show EJ I still cared. I often felt like I couldn't love him like I should, but tonight I would try. This gesture would show him that yes, I was so focused on my success, listening to these tapes, but that didn't mean I didn't have time for him.

I parked in front of the restaurant and there he was: but he wasn't alone. As I unbuckled my seatbelt, I saw him near the massage parlor section of the parking lot. Miss Scraggle Hair was embracing him by the waist. Her breasts pressed against his chest. Then they kissed each other. Fuming, I threw the car into reverse and headed home.

In the morning as I got ready for work, EJ had been dropped off on our doorstep. I was dressed in a suit while he reeked of body odor and pepperoni, still wearing his day-old, white button up shirt with the pizza joint logo and jeans. Standing in the foyer together, we couldn't have looked more different —or been in more different places. I crossed my arms as he began to fumble for a winning excuse for being out all night.

"Pizza delivery people don't work *that* late," I said. "I know where you were. I know that your co-worker, Harry, lied for you and you weren't fixing a car, so spare me the lie."

EJ kept looking down and shuffling his feet.

I finally burst. "How could you do this to me?" I said. "I'm working so hard!"

I was trying to better my life. Why wasn't he doing the same thing? That's when I watched his eyes change and his arms were in the air.

"You don't have any time for me," he said. "All you care about is building a business and making money! It's all about Shaena and painting. Where do I fit into that?"

For some reason, I understood: I hadn't been there for him. He was looking for the companionship he couldn't find at home. Tears formed in my eyes.

In some ways, I was relieved. Clearly, we had nothing in common, and I needed to stay focused on my career. I could take care of Shaena on my own, because I already was anyway. Maybe it was time to part ways, and that's why I said what I said next: "I understand; I'm a failure for not having time for you," I said. "It's best if you go now."

EJ furrowed his eyebrows. He expected a fight full of jealousy and instead received a ticket to freedom. "I don't want it to be like this," he said. "I love you, and I want you to be there for me."

"I can't," I said. "I need to focus on our daughter and live my dream. The only way to do that is to build my business. We're in two different places."

I stormed into the bedroom of our little country farmhouse and started taking his clothes out of the bureau and throwing them into a trash bag. I started hyperventilating and there was nothing he could say to slow me down.

"Angel, you gotta calm down," he said, crying.

"I don't blame you for what you did," I said. "I get it, but you got to get your stuff and go. You can't be with other people while you're here."

I handed him the trash bag.

"I wish you wouldn't be like this," he said. "You don't have to be so cold."

Keeping my face as emotionless as I could, I said, "I understand it's my fault and I can't be there like you need me, but I need to build some kind of future for myself and Shaena."

After wavering in the doorway, he walked out.

"Go, you gotta go," I said as he walked down the driveway.

He had no other choices with me.

And he left.

When EJ left, I had to get even more focused. I was so used to people leaving my life that I had to keep moving. No time to mourn. EJ had taken our only car and left, so I couldn't get to work. I called down to the pizzeria and told the owner, Sal, to come pick me up in his brown van. Instead, he sent Harry. With some trepidation, I got into the car and was silent on the way to the club. I wanted him to say something about EJ, why he had stood up for someone who was lying.

I didn't have to wait long.

"I'm sorry I lied about where EJ was," he said. "I did it because he seemed so unhappy."

"Well, I don't blame you," I said. "I understood why he did it."

I tried to put in one of my books on tape and he blocked me. "School's over for now," he said. He started playing the Isley Brothers, Led Zeppelin, and Robert Plant. Suddenly, I was having fun with this guy. I usually wasn't so relaxed. Harry was fun, and life wasn't about studying day and night, or working 24/7. I seemed to forget all about my tapes.

Maybe EJ had been right; I'd been too serious and wrapped up in my work. I needed to let my hair down, and Harry seemed to be the right person to let me chill out for once.

At the end of the day, we parked back at my house, and started dancing around under the blue moon. The moon was so huge and it felt like our bodies were lit under the moonlight. Harry drove me to a bar. A 20-year-old woman and a 31-year-old man in a bar. We danced under the lights, and I felt myself drawn into his dark eyes. He was hyper, more in my energy than EJ. With his leather jacket and slicked back, black hair and charcoal-colored eyes. I hadn't gone out in months, and I was out during my painting hours. And I was actually enjoying myself.

He even started howling at the moon—literally howling at the moon, and I laughed. And then we locked eyes. It was a crisp, cool March morning, and in that moment, we became magnets to each other. I looked up into his eyes and our lips were close together. I almost didn't understand the butterflies in my stomach, but I recognized that this was one of the moments people talk about. The ones you see in the movies. And we kissed.

A few months later, Harry insisted on throwing me a twenty-first birthday party with my family. He spent $200 and built a grill overnight in the backyard of my country-style house, which was a twenty-minute drive from the city where we both worked. Under a moon that wasn't quite as blue or large or romantic as that one night, I sipped beer and watched Harry talk with my uncle, who would watch Shaena along with a few of the upstairs neighbors when I was at work. As I stood observing them, my uncle started to tense up. Harry looked like he was trying to make himself bigger, getting a little too close to my uncle's face. I put down my beer and walked over.

"What's happening here?" I asked.

"Your uncle seems to think I'm not good enough," he said, slurring his words. His breath reeked of alcohol and his body barreled toward me. "I stayed up all night long getting your birthday together. Aren't you happy with it?"

I froze, looking into the eyes I thought were so romantic before. "Calm down, Harry," I said. "We don't have to be like this at my birthday party."

My uncle stepped in between us. As he did, Harry punched him in the face. I screamed, and the other people at the party gasped and looked at us. My uncle held his chin, covered in blood, and looked at Harry with an incredulous expression. I threw my beer on the ground.

"Get out of here, Harry," I said, fuming.

The next morning, Harry's car was gone. I figured he got a ride home since he was drunk, but that wouldn't explain why his car was missing. He would be back to pick up his car and take me to work. I waited for twenty minutes and checked my watch, having already dropped off Shaena with my uncle upstairs. Thankfully, he didn't need stitches. I was going to tell Harry he couldn't do what he did again. That he wasn't allowed to just punch out my family members at a party he insisted on throwing for me. But after forty-five minutes, I went back inside and called the pizzeria.

"Did Harry show up for work?" I asked. "I'm here at home and I don't have a ride."

"No, I have no idea where he is," said Sal.

We started calling the local police stations. Nothing.

"I'll come pick you up," said Sal. About twenty minutes later, he arrived in a beat up, chocolate brown utility van. It had dents all over it and it sounded like the van was sputtering as it chugged down the road. *Dunt, dunt, dunt.* There were papers all over the passenger footwell that I had to step around as I got into the seat.

When we got to the pizzeria, the phone rang and Sal picked up. His face went from neutral to concerned as he said very little as he listened. I lingered, having this feeling it had something to do with Harry. When he hung up, Sal shook his head. "He's in jail," he said. "Apparently, he drove home drunk last night and got arrested."

Great, I thought sarcastically.

"But if you need to use the van for a while, that's fine," said Sal.

The silver lining to Harry being in jail was that my head was suddenly free again to focus on my goals: being a great mom to Shaena and listening to my tapes that kept me sane and grounded in myself. The beat up brown van that Sal lent me had a tape player, so I could finally get back to my tapes after not being able to listen to them when I was riding with Harry. I put in one of Harry's tapes, the *Pretty in Pink* soundtrack, when I needed a break from healing my inner child or parenting tips. I'd put that in, open the window with its hand crank, and sing at the top of my lungs. I could barely hear the music because the car was so loud with its muffler sputtering.

But it didn't matter. I was independent again.

On a wintry Saturday night months later, I was listening to the weather report on the radio in the back of the Kauna Club. The music pulsed on the dance floor as I heard about the ice warning taking effect until tomorrow morning at 9:00 a.m. *We'd have to close early*, I thought, *just to be safe*. I let the DJ know what was happening and we began closing the bar. I threw on my red leather jacket and headed outside to the van. I played "Pretty in Pink" as I drove down the road. I had to drive up a mountain called Space Mountain to get home. The song played as I kept inching higher and higher up the mountain.

Suddenly, the wheels spun out of control. The van lurched. I must have hit a patch of ice, and I swerved into a tree. I was thrown through the windshield right before the engine hurtled forward, crushing the driver's seat where I would have been sitting. I laid on the ice-covered ground, faintly hearing the sirens of an ambulance.

A paramedic shone a light into my face. I was too weak to move my hands in front of my face. They picked me up carefully and placed me on a stretcher to take me to the hospital. Glass shards stuck to every part of my body, including my face. I watched the paramedic about to slice off my leather jacket. "No, please, don't," I said faintly, but he did it anyway, attaching me to an IV and whatever other wires and tubes that were going to save my life. I couldn't see out of my left eye, and passed out.

In the hospital, I fell into a coma. While I was out, I was pumped with all kinds of medicine to decrease my swelling. Powerful drugs. About two months later, I woke up to see a nurse checking my vital signs. A doctor came to my side and began telling me what was happening. I had more than 200 stitches in my face, on the outside and inside from one side of my forehead to the other. The bones under my eye, my forehead, and my nose were shattered. I had a horrible concussion and my frontal lobe was damaged. But the doctor was also telling me something else. I had to ask what he was saying over and over again until I understood.

"Angel, you're three months pregnant," the doctor said.

I winced in pain. "What?" I asked.

"Yes, but we found out after we'd given you medications to ease your pain," said the doctor. "We're afraid this will lead to the baby having deformities."

"I'm having this baby," I said. "And I accept the responsibility of it. This baby is going to be OK and God is going to help me."

Then, Thelma ran into the room, looking scared but relieved. I had no idea how long she'd been in the hospital, when she'd found out, or even if I was really awake. I felt like I'd been passed out either for years or one minute, no in between. "I'm ready to leave," I said once I saw Thelma, hoping she'd grab my things and we'd go. Thelma grabbed my hand and looked into my eyes as if she had been keeping track of my progress while I had been asleep.

"It's OK, Angel," she said. "Do what you think is best."

I looked at the doctor and back at Thelma. Maybe I hadn't realized I was three months pregnant between the long hours I was working and being in a coma. But I wasn't about to let go of a life that was growing inside of me. I didn't care. I was going to have this baby.

"Do you think I should have this baby, Thelma?" I said.

She squeezed my hand. "You do what's best for yourself," she said.

I was fine with the risk. "All right," I said, and I signed the hospital release of liability form, absolving them of any responsibility for potentially harming my unborn child.

The doctors had to do reconstructive surgery on my face. Four reconstructive surgeries to be exact, and I still couldn't open my eyelid for almost six months afterward. I couldn't live on my own anymore, and needed constant care that exceeded what my uncle and neighbors could handle. Thelma packed me a bag and drove me to the one place I didn't want to go, but seemingly had no choice: back to Mom, Thelma and Bernie's house. I had no idea why I was back here, but I was hoping Thelma would tell me since I was starting to get nervous.

Thelma settled me into a couch in a quiet room of the house where I could shut the curtains and be in complete darkness. I writhed in pain from severe headaches and got dizzy just from sitting up too fast. My face felt cold to the bone. She left for several minutes and returned with a tray. "Time to have some lunch," she said.

I pushed it away. "I wanna go home," I said, rolling over.

"Angel, you don't live there anymore," she said.

I struggled to sit up, but this seemed important. "What do you mean? I've paid the rent on time, every time. I was just there."

"You've been out of that house for three months while you were in the coma," said Thelma. "They evicted you."

Stunned, I put my head in my hands. The one place I'd made for myself was gone. At least I had my job. When would I go back to work?

"Can you drive me to the ad agency tomorrow?" I said. "I have a lot to catch up on."

Just then, EJ came through the door. They shared a knowing silence, like they had already told me this news before and for some reason I wasn't remembering. "You're suffering from short-term memory loss, sweetie," said EJ. "You need to take it easy and let us take care of you."

"Where is Shaena?" I asked.

"She's in the living room with your mom," said Thelma. "She's fine."

That's when I lurched up. No. No. Shaena shouldn't be spending that much time with mom. "I'm gonna leave," I said, frantic, "I've gotta get out of this house." I felt like something bad was going to happen. The sound grated on every one of my senses. I gotta get out of here.

I was being sucked back in. Just like I was back in Dunkle Street. But I had no bike to help me escape my mother. With all of my strength, I sat up, feeling the weight of my head as if it was a bowling ball. I opened the door, squinting my eyes at the light streaming in, and saw Shaena sitting in Mom's lap. Mom was feeding her candy with the same expression on her face that she had when she fed nuts to Chatty the squirrel. I had a sense of jealousy, like I wish I could fit in with them. I wish I could be a part of this family. It seemed like everyone could connect with each other. While EJ was talking with Mom and Shaena was giggling, I felt like I was in the way. It felt like my mom was trying to take away my family. If Shaena started loving my mom, would she love her more than me? The worst feeling would be losing my daughter's love. I'd learned how to love her and now it was going to be taken away. I started to panic. When Mom came in with Shaena, my daughter looked up and stared at me. I extended my arms and tried to smile, even though it hurt my face.

"Shaena, come here," I said. She didn't move. It was clear I was back to abiding by Mom's rules and losing control of the life I'd carefully built.

I was like one of her children again.

Chapter 8

Blistering migraines became my new normal. I would wake up to the sliver of sun that came through the blackout curtains in my mom's guest room, and it tore my brain apart. Each morning I winced, looked around, and sadly remembered I was in Mom's house.

For those keeping score, I'd been:

Evicted from the home I worked so hard to keep.

Forced to live with my mom who was turning my own daughter against me.

And asked to sign hospital paperwork acknowledging my child could be born with birth defects. A child that, as far as EJ knew, came out of nowhere. I'd hid from the truth myself, the coma a shield from what my heart knew: that Sal had been more than my ride.

As if he could read my thoughts, EJ came into the room holding a tray with breakfast: scrambled eggs, sausage patty, and an orange. He seemed so happy to be caring for me. I witnessed the adoration in his eyes and how much he seemed to care. His words still full of concern for me. I felt so helpless in getting out of this situation, repeating the cycles of where I was. I'd heard him and my mom laughing together, building a relationship, and he was the only one able to work and make money.

Why was he helping me?

I didn't deserve him.

Maybe I didn't even deserve my daughter.

"I'm not mad, you know," he said as he put a napkin on my lap. "I had to know you would move on. But I'm still here and I'm not going anywhere again."

He was talking about my being four months pregnant, a fact I re-pieced together each morning. I nodded at his seemingly generous admission.

"I appreciate that," I said, taking a bite of my eggs. "We'll get through this together." I was still worried everyone would take away everything I'd worked for.

Each day, I tried to paint again. I'd put up an easel and mix colors in a palette. Searching the painting, I wondered where I was going to put the paint, and suddenly I didn't remember. My left eye was barely able to open as I tried to look deeply into the blank canvas. This warm, melting feeling inside my head persisted, and nothing made sense to me. My pictures of yellow daisies, the color of my old bike on Dunkle Street, were my compass. I put the golden color in the middle and started painting the petals. *Wait, what was I doing*? I went to clean my brush out and mixed another color for another part of the flower. Then I stopped.

What am I doing right now?

Oh, I'm trying to paint.

Why were the petals yellow? Shouldn't they be white?

I took my knee and nudged up the middle of the easel, pushed my hand in the middle of where the painting was and smudged the flower. I couldn't even paint a daisy. I kicked the easel. Anger seethed through me, then a scream. The sharp pain in my knee was nothing compared to the pain in my head. Then I flew into a rage.

Why can't I do this?

My short-term memory was fading.

I could remember the yellow from Dunkle Street.

But I couldn't remember how to paint a daisy. My brain felt like it was stuck in sludge, unable to do what I loved and usually knew so well.

EJ and Sal were far from the only men in my life, whether I wanted them to be or not. I gave birth to my son Billy about five months later. Afterward, EJ volunteered to put his name on the birth certificate even though he was absolutely in no way Billy's biological dad. He accepted the responsibility in the same hospital where I had fallen into a coma almost a year beforehand. He took it up like a mantle. When little Billy was born, he was yellow with a bluish tint, as if he wasn't getting enough oxygen. His skin was so tight. When I pinched his arm, I couldn't feel the body fat. He wasn't loose and soft like a regular baby.

I had to do exercises with him to loosen up his body. He screamed a lot even when he came home, and he was always jumping, which caused a lot of tension between EJ and me.

EJ got us an apartment away from my mom. I was finally able to get work in the UPS overnight packaging department. I was feeling better and grateful for the love and support EJ had given me to get us back on our feet. I was slowly gaining my freedom back. EJ was working a lot as he was going back-and-forth to Philly. Sometimes only coming home on the weekends, it was clear we were growing apart. We were right back where we started, fighting and not seeing each other.

"We're not happy," I said, and he agreed, moving back to Philly. I was living in the apartment by myself with the kids, getting help from a babysitter. When I went over to the pizza joint one afternoon, I saw the familiar, intoxicating leather jacket and slicked back hair: Harry. He was out of prison, and I was drawn in all over again.

"Hey, how are you?" I said.

His lips turned up in this irresistible way. "Hey, did you miss me?" he said almost sarcastically, as if he'd never been to prison at all. "I heard you had a kid."

"Yep," I said.

He went outside and picked up a little spider off of a fake web that had been put up for Halloween and handed it to me. "Here's a little something for him," he said. I furrowed my eyebrows.

Oh, did he think Billy was his?

"How about you come over, I'll make you dinner and you can fix my stereo?"

He beamed. "Sure, I'll be there."

I heard a car outside and looked through the curtains. Sal was in the driver's seat, and Harry hopped out of the passenger's side. When the doorbell rang, my stomach fluttered with the memories of what we had under the full moon years ago. When I opened the door, I was almost mad at myself for taking in that leather jacket, slicked back hair, and grimace of a smile. This was not someone who deserved second chances, and yet something was drawing me right back into howling-at-the-moon Harry. I could barely speak when I looked at him.

"Come in," I stammered. "I made meatballs."

He walked into the kitchen and saw that they had raisins in them, like the meatballs he used to make. He was far from being Italian, but took up the culture as his own. Looking inside the pot, he saw the raisins. "You didn't do half-bad there, girl," he said.

The fluttering in my stomach continued. He lifted up my cheek with his finger and I turned my head, and landed on his lips. I felt like melted butter in his hands.

After dinner, Harry and I sat on the edge of my bed as he tinkered with my stereo, and I tried not to ask him what jail was like. I wanted to know but thought he was probably getting enough of that. When he looked at me, I felt that familiar surge of electricity. Of freedom.

"So you named him Billy, huh?" he said with a deep breath.

My heart started pounding.

"Oh, do you think that Billy is your kid?" I said, shaking at the thought of how I was going to have to explain to him what happened.

Then I told him the full story. His face fell a little, but didn't change his emotional high from us reconnecting again. He kept working on the stereo. "It doesn't matter whether I'm on the birth certificate or not" he said. "We still got our spark." He grabbed me by the waist and kissed me deeply.

Then, he went into his overnight bag, which he always carried around with him. He pulled out the cassette tape of the Isley Brothers' song, "Between the Sheets." With a knowing smile, he popped it into the stereo and the song began bouncing off the walls. I fell into it.

I reached out for his hand and he immediately took it in his. Feeling so safe with him, I just knew Harry was going to make everything better. My life with him would be good.

"Angel, I swear to you, I'm going to do better from now on," said Harry. "No more drinking, no more drugs, just going to do right by you and your kids."

And that was all I needed to hear. We were going to be a little family, at last.

Harry and I started officially dating again. Since he was living in Little Italy near the pizza joint, he invited me to come over and live with him. Little did I know that Sal, Billy's biological dad, arranged for all of it. He kept an eye on his son and me while Harry started right back working with him. As Harry went inside to start making pizzas, I saw Sal looking at me a little longer than usual, maybe not at me. Maybe behind me at the dark-haired, smiling, three-month-old boy in the car seat. It had been a year, but maybe he was surprised to see me finally driving a car again.

About ten months later, I was reading my Bible at night. Harry was going to AA and I was going to Al-Anon. I was also eight months pregnant with his child. All seemed good. But one night, Harry came home from work and I gave him a huge hug. That's when I smelled the Coors Light on his breath.

"I thought you gave up drinking," I said.

He waved me away. "Not much, babe," he said, annoyed. "I worked all day."

I let it go, and engrossed myself in my own work, unwilling to get into a fight with him about his drinking. I took up painting and listening to books on tape. It would all be fine.

Another night when I was reading, I knew Harry would be home soon from hanging out with his friends, friends I hadn't met yet. The kids were safely asleep and there was nothing to worry about except which show I'd watch next.

Then I saw the headlights of Harry's car beam through the window curtains. A door thrust open and slammed closed. I could hear the crunch of the driveway gravel under his boots and the piercing twist of his keys into the lock. He burst into the foyer, the smell of whiskey following him a little too closely. He threw his jacket on the floor, revealing a bloodied white t-shirt. His eyes looked huge.

"It looks like a whorehouse in here," he said, his eyes darting around at the laundry I hadn't folded yet. *Whorehouse? Hardly.* I stood up, my pregnant belly jutting into the middle of the room as I put my hands on my hips. "What's going on?" I asked. He began walking toward me, menacing, looking like he'd never met me in our lives. He reeked of gasoline, booze, cigarettes, the whiff of charred flames.

When we were eye-to-eye, he grabbed the back of my head, and pulled it back as taut as a rubber band and launched me into the opposite wall. The thud made my vision go blurry, and I fell to the ground, stunned. He picked me up by the same spot again and hurled me into another wall. The shape of my head was in three different parts of the wall. My head went straight through the drywall. Then he left me on the ground, blood seeping from my scalp.

He threw everything at me: paint, brushes, and my easel, flipping end tables over my back. He broke a lamp over my back. I tried to protect my belly. The rage and his rambling of his words meant I couldn't understand what he was saying. He talked about fire. An alleged robbery. The look in his eyes was blank and empty—that of a crazy person. He was unrecognizable. It was like looking into the eyes of the devil. He lifted a bat over my head as I was lying down.

"You see this bat?" he said. "You're gonna get splattered if you move. I dare you to move your head or you're gonna get a good look at this bat."

Then he went into the kitchen to make a call.

"Do you think they got us?" said Harry. "Do you think they got the license plate?"

Then he listened.

"Alright, we gotta get out of here," he said. "I don't see it on the news, but we just gotta get out of here until this cools off."

I was scared to death of Harry, frozen in place and unable to call 911 or help myself in any way. I kept my eyes open all night. My head was swollen and raced. He was asleep next to me, and I thought about escaping. Where would I go? He had the only vehicle, so I couldn't take his car and leave. I was a prisoner.

The next morning, I called Bernie and asked her to fetch Shaena and Billy. Bernie winced and looked concerned, but unfortunately she was used to me looking beat up. Sheree hurt me. Now Harry hurt me. I knew she wasn't the kind of person to get involved, as she always was when it came to my mom. Mom didn't seem to care at all. She was busy cooing with Harry, which she always did with my boyfriends. She laughed and tapped his arm, and I felt the rage roil through me.

At least Bernie wanted to say something about my head.

"Are you ok?" she whispered.

"I'm fine," I said as I handed Billy to her. Then all four of them left, leaving me with Harry, who stood in the back watching. He was fast talking. "Everything's good," he said. "We need a break and just need to go to the ocean. Thanks so much for helping out." I closed my eyes. I'd rather stay here with Harry than go back to Mom's apartment. Thelma lived in the same building in another apartment, and I thought about going there. But in the end, I chose Harry. I was just hoping Bernie and Mom would take the kids and not ask any more questions.

Then we set off for the beach. Which beach, I had no idea.

I placed a cooler in the back of the car, and that's when I noticed a grungy, head-banging man with greasy blonde hair coming up the driveway. He was dead in the eyes and looked like a devil worshipper. "Trevor," said Harry. "You think they got our plates?"

"Nah, bro," said Trevor. "We gotta get out of here."

Then Trevor looked at me.

"I don't need to go with you," I said.

He shook his head. Harry didn't want to let me out of his sight, and I was his permanent tagalong. When you're with someone who scared you to death, you did what they said.

"No way," said Trevor. "Get your fucking ass in the backseat." He lunged toward me and shoved me against the car door of the Mercury Grand Marquis. In the back passenger's seat, I was squashed against the Styrofoam cooler filled with beers. White hot fear seized my insides. They slammed their car doors shut, Harry in the front seat, Trevor shotgun.

"It's gonna be a long drive," said Harry. "Babe, hit me with a beer."

I paused.

"Babe, give me a fucking beer!"

I whipped the cooler open and shakily passed him a Coors Light. He took a gulp, started the engine, and went on to drive for eight terrifying hours. With each car that we passed, I thought about knocking on my window. *Help me*, I wanted to mouth. *Help me get out of this car.* But what if Harry saw me doing that? Or Trevor? I especially had no idea what Trevor was capable of as I watched him whittle a once whole toothpick into a splinter with his teeth.

We arrived in Ocean City, Maryland. A long stretch of light orange sand met the gray-blue water of the ocean. Harry parked the car and leapt out, and Trevor followed. For five minutes, I heard the ringing of silence in my ears. Perhaps they would leave me here while they did whatever they came here to do. But then I heard the click of the trunk opening, and I saw Harry in the rearview mirror pulling out a tent I didn't even know was in the car. We'd bought that tent to go look at the stars, or a full moon, like the evening we'd fallen for each other.

The howl-at-the-moon kind of attraction we felt.

But now I was covered in bruises.

Then my door opened.

"Get out," Harry said. I followed him and Trevor to Jolly Roger Pier. There was something in me that was dizzy, unsteady as I walked along the pier. Sweat glued my bangs to my forehead. I could taste the saltiness of sweat in my mouth. It felt like there was a rock in my stomach, and it was solid. Dizzy, I walked by sandcastles on the ocean. One depicted *The Last Supper*. I stumbled out of the car and saw the man making the castle. He was doing something for God. He had to have faith. He pointed toward his can for donations.

His energy reminded me of Mr. Stacks.

He had to help me.

"Please help me," I pleaded. "I can't feel my baby moving."

I felt a hard hand on my arm and then took me into their arms, trying to make it look like a hug. "Get back here," said Harry. "What the fuck are you trying to do?" The man just watched me as Harry dragged me away. We drove to a campground in Delaware Beach and set up the tent there.

The next morning, I woke up feeling warm, dark blood near my pelvis. My head was swimming in addition to my usual blinding migraine, and I started saying Harry's name to wake him up, even though I was scared to do that. I didn't have any other choice. I woke him up and noticed that he was also covered in blood. I was having contractions and screaming.

"I think I'm losing the baby," I said. "I'm not supposed to be bleeding this much."

Sitting in a puddle of blood, Harry knew we had to do something.

"Ok, ok," he said. "I'll get you to the hospital." He drove me to Bee's Hospital while Trevor was still sleeping in the tent. When he was away from Trevor, his face softened, realizing what was happening: That we were losing our child together. I was going in and out of consciousness, my eyes fluttering, slipping away into the dark and then waking up.

Once we got into the ER, I was rushed into a room. Because I was having little contractions, they put the monitor on my belly.

"There's no heartbeat," the doctor said to the nurse.

"She's not dilated," said a nurse. "Let's keep trying."

As I felt myself giving birth, there were no cries ricocheting off the hospital walls. No relief from the labor I had endured. The doctor solemnly showed me my baby: she was thoroughly purple, dark. She didn't move. My body started shaking, and my only witness to my building grief was the hospital staff.

"I'm so sorry," I said, crying. A strange sense of relief was mixed in, knowing I could love a daughter, but I couldn't bring her into this situation. She was so heavy in my arms. I felt so bad for her and was really scared. I didn't really know what to do.

"You're going to need some blood," said the doctor. "We'll do whatever you want us to do. Do you want us to take her?"

Weeping, I handed her to them. There was nothing else for me to do.

"Please take her," I said, choking on my tears. The doctor lingered, patting me on the shoulder. I could see him looking over my bruises. He gently touched my arm.

"Were you in a car accident?" he asked. I could tell he was suspicious.

"Oh no," I said, my eyes still full of tears.

The doctor nodded, and asked me a few routine questions before leaving the room.

Harry looked relieved that I hadn't said what happened to me. But his eyes narrowed, as if he felt the doctor was on to him. He couldn't risk them finding out he had beaten me.

"Angel, we gotta go," he said.

"My daughter's in the other room and I just can't leave."

He put his hand over the top of my arm and pulled out the IV. He had a change of clothes for me.

"OK, come on," he said. "If you don't get your stuff, you're staying here."

As I lay there, my face stained with tears, I wondered if this could be my out. This might be my only opportunity to leave Harry and start a safer, healthier life. A lightness came to my heart: could this be the freedom I desperately needed? As fast as the idea came to me, it left even faster: who would take care of my kids? I had to go back home and protect them not just from Harry, but my mom. I didn't trust anyone but myself to care for them.

Defeated, I allowed Harry wrap the gauze around my arm, covering up traces of the IV he had ripped out moments earlier. We walked out of the room without telling anyone. Trevor was already in the car ready to go. I had no words. I had no way of communicating except for the tears in my eyes and grief that twisted my mouth.

We walked through the double doors and we were gone.

No one could even see that I was a patient in the room.

Once again I was trapped by the cooler, which made a *slooshing* sound each time we hit a bump in the road or Harry would pound on the breaks. My baby, purple and lifeless and without a name, was gone. Left in Ocean City. I didn't even get to say goodbye.

"Beer me, Angel," said Harry.

As I touched the cold, wet beer bottle, I started whimpering. I convulsed inside and was too afraid to cry out loud, but it kept seeping out of me in other sounds. There was something about the coldness of the beer that reminded me of the cold railing of the hospital bed where I had given birth to my stillborn daughter. Something broke inside of me and I couldn't say anything.

"You know, I don't think they recognized us," said Trevor. "I bet they won't even recognize us if we go back."

"We shouldn't have given that guy a ride," said Harry.

Trevor sneered. "We showed him, bro," he said. "And I think we're cool."

So Harry and Trevor lit someone on fire? I still wasn't sure. This time I didn't even look out the window or ask for help. What I had become, and what I didn't realize at the time, was the woman in the bolero jacket on the Atlantic City pier. The woman who met a well-dressed man and went to a house for a party only to find out she would be tied to a bed and abused with no hope of help coming to save her.

I was alone. I was ashamed of myself. I knew Mr. Stacks was looking down and wasn't proud of me at all. I wondered if my stillborn daughter was with Pops, and if he was holding her with the love he had. As I looked out the window, I wished I hadn't learned to love this deeply in Denny's with Mr. Stacks, passing Shaena back-and-forth. I closed my eyes and began to pray. *Lord, please let my daughter be in Mr. Stacks' arms, and be at peace as he is in heaven. I'm not a bad person and will regret what happened to her every day of my life. But, Lord, you have to know that I couldn't bring a baby into this kind of world where I was a prisoner in my own life.* I opened my eyes again, and realized I was relieved and sad at the same time.

And frightened.

No one was coming to save me.

Chapter 9

After I returned home, my nightmare in Ocean City refused to fade over the next week. I tried to stay focused on getting healthier so I could pick up my kids from Bernie's and Mom's, but everything reminded me of the child I left at the hospital. I'd see my daughter's hairbrush in the bathroom and yearn to feel the downy softness of my stillborn girl's hair nestled between my fingers. I yearned to smell that soft, lavender and honey-esque baby smell, to feel the softness of her soft arms and chubby legs. The cold fear of holding her lifeless body made me sob. I repeated my prayer to Mr. Stacks in those moments.

I was thinking about this on loop as Harry and I slept, or at least as he slept and I pretended to close my eyes. Then, I heard a loud, horrible banging. Jumping out of bed, I thought something had happened to a neighbor. I tiptoed to the front door and peered through the peephole. Seven cops were lined up, looking around as if they were being casual, but their drawn guns were anything but.

"Harry, there are a bunch of cops outside!" I said.

I heard his feet hit the hard wooden floors and he ran up to me.

"Don't open the door," he said, his expression dark and insistent. He put his hands on my shoulders and looked at me intensely. "Just don't."

But the police weren't going to take a closed door as an answer.

BAM. BAM. BAM.

"One minute," I said, so I could unlock the door from the right side, still wanting to protect my belly, which was still feeling tender and empty.

Harry fled into the bedroom while I stood there frozen, watching this cascade of black uniforms stream into my home. "What happened?!" I asked.

The police officer leading the charge asked, "Is Harry Smith here?"

I went to say something, but they were already down the hall. That's when I started screaming. The kids were still with Bernie and Mom, and I was thankful I hadn't picked them up yet, even though I never thought this would happen. Harry flailed as he tried to get out of bed, but he only made it into the bathroom when the seven police officers grabbed him and threw him back on the bed. They read him his Miranda rights and cuffed him.

"What the hell did I do?" he asked.

"Do you know Trevor Brown?" the police said. "You're under arrest for attempted murder."

I gasped. They stood Harry up and maneuvered his head forward as they walked. So the news reports were true: a man alongside the road ran out of gas. He was holding a gas can, and Harry and Trevor decided to pick him up and take him to the gas station. As the man was about to pay for the gas, Harry and Trevor saw the wad of cash in his hand. While they drove him back to his car, they decided to rob him. The man tried to defend himself by throwing gasoline on them, and then Harry and Trevor took the can and poured it on him, robbed him and tried to set him on fire with a cigarette lighter. The man was still in the hospital in critical condition.

"Angel, call Sal," he said in a pressured voice. "Let him know they're taking me!"

As I watched the police load Harry into the back of the squad car, I felt a massive sense of relief. I sat down in my living room, closed my eyes, and soaked up the silence. The police didn't ask me any questions and were like a SWAT team, intent on getting him. I continued to sit alone for two more days, feeling parts of myself that had died begin to at least start to heal. Then I called my mom and told her it was time to pick up the kids. It was as if God had protected my children from seeing Harry get arrested. A small miracle in a week that felt like hell.

Over the next six months, Harry kept trying to call me from jail. I was hoping he'd stay there for awhile, but with each attempted call, it felt like the police were beating down my door all over again. I made four court appearances on his behalf, and with each appearance I wondered why I was still defending someone who had hurt me so badly.

After one of the last court appearances, Sal called. His voice sounded angry with a tinge of relief after I told him what happened. "Geez, Angel," he said. "I'm glad you're ok, but I hate that Harry did that to you." Then he paused. "I heard he's getting out on that 50,000-dollar bail. I rather you hear it from me first than someone else."

I didn't understand why they were letting him out on bail. How could anyone who would do something so heinous get out so quickly?

"You have some time," said Sal. "I can come over and give you a ride to work."

Sal came over a couple of hours later. When I opened the passenger side door, he gave me a concerned smile. "How you holding up, Angel?" he asked as I buckled my seatbelt. I could feel him staring at the sadness in my eyes. We looked at each other, and I could feel a rush of calm come over me. He made me feel safe.

When we arrived at Sal's pizza joint, we looked at each other again, deeply, wantonly. Going into the pizza joint, he and I seemed to have an understanding of where we wanted to go, and for us it was a familiar place, the same place we had brought Billy into the world. Sal took my hand and led me into his office with a soft, strong gaze in his eyes. I shut the door behind me and fell into his warm, brown eyes.

I embraced him and cried softly into his shoulder.

"I was so scared," I whispered to him. He wrapped his arms around me, enveloping me in his musk, which was a mixture of cologne and warm bread.

"You're safe with me," he said.

We kissed as if I was a desert and he was a glass of cold water. In my own way, I wanted to thank him for saving me, for loving me, and I wanted to return the favor. Showing love with sex had always been something I did, and it felt right to reward Sal with this for all he had done for me. We shoved papers off of his small wooden desk as we kissed and tore off each other's clothes. I was eager to once again feel that pump of protective, loving feelings.

With Harry in jail before his arraignment, I took up new, healthier hobbies. I'd get up every morning and go for a run, while my neighbor watched the kids. It reminded me of the freedom I had riding my bike on Dunkle Street. It felt so good that I signed up for a marathon. I worked out so much that I didn't realize my period hadn't been arriving like it did. When I looked at myself in the mirror, I noticed my belly button seemed to protrude. My nipples were darker and bigger. While my mind knew what all of these symptoms could mean, I didn't focus on it.

After multiple arraignments to lower his bail, Harry got out. I was in the living room, waiting for Harry to come back. I'd take a deep breath and hoped that he would be put away for a long time. But he was just getting out on bail and I would need to still live with him until his arraignment, which could be months away. I moved things around the living room. I cleaned floors, washed dishes, anything to keep my mind busy. Then I heard that familiar sound of a car pulling into the gravel driveway. Sal had picked him up from jail.

The keys in the lock made my heart sink, and I swallowed hard as he came into the foyer. He was in the same outfit he'd been arrested in. He went straight into the bedroom, so I followed him, not because I desperately wanted to talk to him, but it seemed like the right thing to do. For the next few days, I had to stay with Harry wherever he went. Even if I didn't want to leave the house, or had to stay in the house. I became his shadow.

He got to see me run the marathon, and afterward, I saw my belly was getting bigger. The smile on Harry's face when he looked at me gave me bittersweet feelings; he clearly thought this was his child, as he did the night we made meatballs and he fixed my stereo. But once my second son, Jesse, was born and he began to grow, it was clear he had more of a resemblance to the father he shared with my first son Billy: Sal. Harry and I never talked about it.

One night, I was in the shower rinsing off the dirt, grime, and tiredness of the day. Harry was brushing his teeth at the sink. We had been talking about our lives and childhoods earlier in the day, and while I was still scared he would hurt me, I was hoping we could at least learn about each other and perhaps heal in some way. As I poured shampoo into my palm, made a lather, and started working it into my hair, I asked, "So, what's it like?"

"What's what like?" he said, spitting into the sink and wiping his mouth.

"Being in jail," I said.

He smirked. "Really? You want to know what it was like in jail?"

Harry was so angry when he got out of prison, and I was reading self-help books and feeling like if he talked about the experience, he would feel better.

"Well, I'm just curious," I said.

He put down his toothbrush with a clinking sound, and then held onto each end of the sink while looking into the mirror. "Alright," he said in a low, sinister voice. I continued to lather my hair with a sense the energy in the room had changed as he stepped away from the sink and came to the glass shower door. Although he'd brushed his teeth, he reeked of booze. He'd been drinking before we were supposed to go visit my dad.

My heart beat faster and my hands froze in my hair.

"I'll tell you," he said. "Or I can show you."

He was seething with anger, which frightened me. I had no idea what he meant, but it seemed like he knew and I wasn't going to like it. He lunged at me and grabbed my hair, and wouldn't stop as I started to scream. "This is what the fuck prison is like, Angel," he said. He threw me against the tiled showerhead. My gut slammed against the silver metal faucet, against my rib. He slammed an elbow on my back, making me arch back and forced himself into me, thrusting me into the wall. I sobbed on the inside like I had on the drive back from Ocean City.

"I know you were with Sal when I was locked up," he seethed into my ear. "This is what women like you deserve, this is what happens to women who can't keep their legs together."

I was getting the punishment for all of my sins all my life.

This was what I was going to have to put up with.

In this moment, I felt the broken man that he had become. I felt all of the violations that he had ever felt. And I felt all of the violations I'd done to others.

I never cared about my own life.

I had this coming.

This was like all the other times before while living with my mom, including on Dunkle Street. Staying very quiet, I tried to be tough even though I was crying internally. My hands were so pulled back that it felt like the nerves were dead. Finally he lurched off of me, rinsed himself in the shower and left. My legs shook as I crawled into the corner of the shower stall and sobbed, the shower still running on me until the hot water ran out and cold pellets rained down on me. He made me see how much he had been stripped of himself all of his life, and felt all of his pain. I now understood parts of him that I never wanted to know before. My pain all gushed forward again.

This was my life. This was the way it was going to be.

My hands finally started to loosen and I was able to pull myself up again. I managed to get a towel and I put it around myself. I still sat there a little longer. The kids were in the playroom and hopefully didn't hear what had happened. I wish I'd never asked Harry that question. I should have never asked it at all. I was numb all over again. I heard Harry yell at Shaena, saying, "I didn't hurt your fucking mom." Then the door opened and shut.

When I felt it was safe to come outside, I walked into the kitchen, Shaena said, "Mommy, I can't find Billy." I looked everywhere, until I heard a cough from the kitchen. I started opening up cabinets. There was Billy, stuffed in a cabinet. He was probably hiding from Harry, because he was afraid of him.

The pain in my body was too much to take. I didn't want to think of my kids experiencing the same horror I was going through. I sat him on the counter and tried to soothe him. "Don't do that again to Mommy," I said.

A few weeks later, I went to Blockbuster and found meditation DVD's from Dick Sutphen about hypnotherapy, healing, and letting go of trauma. I checked them out and when I got home, discovered that Harry had been sentenced to state prison for five years. I called my friend, Leteshia, and told her everything that had been happening. "What happened to you, Angel, isn't right," said Leteshia, a family friend of mine who was also in some rough relationships. We had been sharing the thread of abuse with each other. She sounded sad for me but determined to get me out of the situation. "We need to get you out of there."

Leteshia had a small, old country house on an acre of land that her husband's family owned. It was where her mother-in-law passed away. She suggested I live there, even though the house was very old. We would go to this house and fix the kitchen, the bedroom, added new drywall, and ran the electricity.

When Harry finally went to prison, Leteshia and Bernie helped me pack everything from Harry's house, and moved my children and me into the farmhouse. As I began to pack up the house, I wondered if I was a good person in anyone's eyes. I was going to do my best to give my kids a better life, so they wouldn't have to worry what would happen to their mom or themselves. My kids deserved so much better. As I packed up the last of the boxes into Bernie's truck, I looked up to the sky and thought about Mr. Stacks. I was going to show him that I was a good mom. My sins might have been too great, but God still loved me and I knew it. Mr. Stacks still loved me too. The last two items I put in the car was my Bible and Marianne Williamson's book on tape, *A Return to Love.*

Once I left my old house, I sighed and felt good about leaving everything behind. I wanted to have a fresh start without Harry. I moved into the farmhouse house and started a new life where no one knew where I was. My mom, Bernie, and Leteshia helped me set up my kitchen and living room.

Leteshia helped me and I would go on to survive and leave everything in the rearview mirror. I could be free from all of the trauma that happened with Harry. Starting over felt like the best option for me, and that's when I made a pact to myself and Leteshia: we would start over. To show how we would do that, we turned up Whitney Houston's "The Greatest Love of All" as loud as we could and sang into hairbrushes to celebrate our new lives. We popped a bottle of pink champagne and poured it into the kids' plastic tumblers because that's all we had. We danced around the newly renovated kitchen, and laughed and hugged each other as we shed a few tears of relief.

Whitney was right.

Leteshia was right.

I was worth more.

I could do more.

I could move on with my life.

Chapter 10

In the new house, I put away most of the memories I had with Harry. Framed photos of him were put in boxes. Mementos, such as his Isley Brothers cassette, went into the attic. I was someone who held onto everything, and although I could have thrown it all out, it felt as though the child I lost might be watching over me. Although it was a horrible memory, I didn't want to forget her. I had nothing to remember her by, so I kept pictures of her father.

After packing away those items, I walked into the kitchen and almost slipped into a small puddle of water near the table. I watched a drip of water start from the ceiling and land in the same puddle. Great, either the ceiling or roof was leaking. Add that to my list of repairs I need to make this week: fix leaky faucet, add more insulation to the attic, replace that broken tile in the bathroom.

When everything was put away and the kids had gone to bed, a feeling of loneliness crept into my heart. Harry was gone, really gone, and I'd likely never see him again unless I made a huge effort. After all he'd done to me—the Ocean City nightmare and him attacking me in the shower—I should have been more relieved. But all that was running through my mind was: I was by myself with my kids in this big wonderful house, but had no one to talk to.

Would I ever find someone to share this home with—or more than a home: a life? I called Leteshia after several moments of staring at the phone. "There's no one else out there for me," I said, knowing it sounded absolutely untrue to an objective ear, but I could hear the whispers inside of me beginning to build. *You're not worth anything. He knows you better than anyone. What's a few bad moments?*

"Angel, you moved into that house for a reason," said Leteshia, breaking my internalized sadness about Harry. "He hurt you and you can do much, much better than him. Remember that."

"You're right," I said. "I know you're right."

As I tried to fall asleep in a bed that was once for two, I wondered which voice would continue to win out: Leteshia telling me what was true, or what my own mind was saying—that I deserved Harry, and when he was out of prison, he would still be the only person who actually got me. Who else would remember howling under the moon or our conversations back-and-forth from the pizza shop? Who would look at me like he wanted to devour and love me at the same time?

I might never find that again.

The next day I went to go pick up the kids from my mom's house, as usual, after a day of painting murals and portraits. When I opened the door, my mom's eye was swollen and purple, her thin smile concealing her pain. "What happened to you, Mom?" I asked, a high-pitched alarm in my voice.

"Oh, it's nothing," she said, waving it away. "I was trying to screw in a lightbulb that was too high up and it hit me in the face. "With Bernie gone, I have to do my own repairs."

Bernie finally had enough of my mom and left a few months before. I only saw her when she came to pick up my laundry, washed, and folded everything, and brought it back since I had been washing my clothes in my own sink. But my mom was far from alone. Behind her shoulder, I could see the outline of her new boyfriend, Steve. He was at least twenty years younger than my mom and had a football player's build. He was at least six feet tall with deep, honey-colored skin. His gaze was stern and I could smell his dirty clothes from the doorway.

Watching my mom choose abusive people to be in her life was the norm. I didn't think much of it, even when I saw the black and blue mark.

"Alright, mom," I said. "You take good care of yourself."

I shook all the way home. *We're not the same,* I told myself. Yes, I had let Harry turn me black and blue, but he had a disease. As usual, my mom was picking the scum of the Earth to hang out with, and alienating Bernie would be the worst thing she'd done. I wasn't like that. I was only thinking about Harry and not actually taking him back into my new, steady life.

I began to make new traditions with my kids. On Sundays, when most families dolloped pancake batter onto a skillet or ate eggs smothered in hollandaise sauce at their favorite brunch places, our tradition was to drive to the pizza shop to visit Uncle Vinny. With Harry behind bars, I felt safe enough to bring my kids over for a slice. I stood at the counter and looked at the topping choices through the clear sneeze guard that smelled like Windex but still had a few finger smudges on it.

As I decided between the pepperoni and veggie, Vinny watched me impatiently. He knew I was going to order several slices in different combinations to appease the kids. "Get the pepperoni," a rough, yet familiar, voice said confidently, as if he had ordered pizza for my family before. I looked up and into the small window behind Vinny: there he was with his slicked back hair, mid-pizza dough toss. His white apron had a few splashes of marinara sauce. I gasped.

"Harry," I said, my voice as elastic as the dough settling over his fists. I didn't know whether to feel nervous or excited. I'd already re-established my household and felt as if I was strong, but I couldn't stop looking into his eyes, his clear, kind eyes without any hint of drunkenness. He was the man I first met, the man under the moon sharing a kiss with me. He was my Harry.

Leteshia's voice kept coming up. *Remember what he did to you.* Yet my own internal voice kept countering, *he had a disease and he looks better now. Can't I at least be a friend to him? He might need a friend after what he went through in prison.* As I kept thinking of these words intermingling with my own reservations, Harry wiped his hands off and came out of the kitchen. Vinny looked at the two of us and said, "I'll take these slices out to the kids."

Vinny didn't want to get involved, and since Sal was his boss, he stayed clear of anything having to do with Sal, Harry, and me. While he'd told me I needed to get out of the situation I was in, I told him that I had no place to go, especially since I couldn't go back to my mom.

"Angel, you look good," Harry finally said.

"And you look better," I said with a smile. "I didn't know you were already out."

Harry bit his lip. "It didn't seem like a good idea to call you."

"Probably not," I said. "So you're back here?"

He shrugged. "I didn't know where else to go."

A silence fell between us. The heat of the pizza wafted up to the glass sneeze guard as we searched each other's expressions for apologies or admissions.

"I'm sorry I put you through all of that," he said. "Things with Trevor got kinda crazy."

I nodded. I waited for him to apologize for what happened in the shower.

"I was horrible to you," he said. "And I've done my time about it. I'm never going to see that guy again and get into anything like that ever again. I can promise you that."

"Listen, I'm doing well, and I want to keep doing well," I said. "But I also need some help. I can't keep up the house all by myself when I'm taking care of the kids. Can you really promise that?"

He smiled slyly. "Can I? I'll show you."

"Good," I said. "I want to go see a counselor about things that happened to me. Do you want to go?"

Leteshia told me that I was too forgiving. These two words rattled in my mind as I opened the door and invited Harry into my home. It felt surreal to see him physically in a space I had designed specifically to escape him. *But this time was different,* I said to myself. I would be his friend and help him get back into the world. He walked through the kitchen and saw the bucket collecting drips of water from the ceiling. He looked up and studied the damp spot.

"You need a new roof," he said. And as easy as it would have been to ask him to fix it, I resisted. Instead, I put my purse over my shoulder and asked, "Are you ready to go?"

We got into my car and drove the twenty-five miles to Dr. Rogers' office, and sat in a waiting room with a fake fern in the corner. Then Dr. Rogers appeared in the doorway. "Angel?"

In her office, we sat down on a couch. We talked about things that had happened to me when I was young. We agreed to be friends and accountable to each other.

"I know I hurt you," said Harry. "It was because of all the drinking."

As we sat next to each other, I could feel as though his hands were going to come over and needle through mine. Not like a friend, but more than that. Like the way we used to be.

"It's time for you both to heal," Dr. Rogers said.

We made an arrangement with the counselor: That we would stay together as long as Harry never hung out with people like Trevor, and that he would never drink again.

When we got back to my house, Harry threw his leather jacket on the couch and stared at me. I should have told him to go. I should have told him we were just being friends. But I didn't.

Forgiving. Too Forgiving.

When I got home from work one evening, I saw Harry on the roof with a victorious look on his face and surrounded by loose shingles that appeared to have been cut and shaped for the specifications of the leak source. "I fixed it!" he said, excited, proud, looking clear-eyed and pleased with himself. I smiled. "That's great, babe!" I said. "Can't wait to see how it looks in the kitchen." On the outside, the roof seemed fixed. As I walked into the kitchen, though, the wet spot remained on the ceiling. You could still see it clearly on the inside even if it looked fixed on the outside. I figured it would dry up soon.

Later that evening, Harry and I sat down and read the Bible together. After about an hour, he closed the book and held both of my hands. "Let's plan for our own kid," he said.

Blindsided, I looked away and then back at him. "Do you really think that's a good idea after all we've been through together? I mean, the roof just started working again today." I smiled at my own small joke. He nodded.

"I think it'd be good for us," he said. "A fresh start and our own baby to love together."

Then he stopped me from saying another word and walked into the bedroom. He stood on the bed while holding a Sharpie, and drew a circle with an H+A on the ceiling. We made a pact that this baby would never see him go to prison.

"Harry!" I said. "I just painted those walls and ceilings!"

"Forget about that for a second," he said. "See what I mean?"

I took a deep breath. "I love the idea," I said, "But it has to be like this: we'll make sure this kid never experiences any of the things you, me, and my kids have had to go through."

Once you met someone like Harry, you loved him, even with his mistakes. He was still a smooth talker. After we agreed to become friends, and then more, he moved in. He played with the kids when he wasn't working at the pizza shop. But he wasn't just a smooth talker: there were flickers of possible change. We were reading the bible together, going to counseling and he was becoming helpful and connected.

Group therapy was where he finally saw me. We sat amongst ten people who'd also been hurt by addiction and violence. People talked about how things affected them. What made us make the choices we did. In that group, I finally had the chance to talk about my sexual abuse as a child and how I dealt with it, as well as how it set me up for abuse as an adult. Being embarrassed was worse for me than being raped, but I finally realized I needed to tell people about my pain. I unfolded a letter I wrote to Harry, and began to hyperventilate and cry as I started to read it. Harry was right in front of me as I struggled to read my own handwriting.

"I loved you, and all I wanted was for us to have a good life together and to be happy, but when you brought Trevor into our lives, everything changed. I know we had a rough start with the drinking and driving, but when you got mixed up with Trevor, it scared me. When you hurt me like that, it made me feel as if I couldn't trust you again. It made me feel unsafe. I was ashamed of myself. Maybe you felt like I deserved what you did to me in the shower, but it wasn't right. I've been hurt so many times."

Harry was very quiet as he listened to my story, and finally grasping the longstanding consequences of his violent actions. He put his hand on my leg as my eyes continued to fill up with tears. "I'm so sorry for what I did to you," he said. "I'll never hurt you again."

We went out to dinner afterward and then drove home. We were sitting in the car reading out of the Bible. We prayed and asked God to take away the pain we caused each other and other people. That we would be able to be better people. For the first time in a long time, we felt as if we were safe with each other and faced the things we created. "If you're going to drink, you'll have to leave," I said to him. "It makes you do terrible things." I tried not to think about the shower and him grabbing my hair and the things he said when he slammed me against the faucet. It was the alcohol.

"I'm done with all that," said Harry, and he held my hand tenderly.

Our son Jeremy was born with a full head of hair and clear, big, black eyes just like Harry's. You couldn't see the difference between his irises and his pupils. For the first time, I was able to say this child had all of his qualities instead of knowing my child had another father. Jeremy further bonded Harry and me together as we built a new life with each other that was based on healing and telling the truth, always.

I got involved in the PTA and started coaching soccer with the kids. Our life began to resemble a stereotypical fairy tale. At an after-school program, the school was talking about Earth week and things we could do. I talked about the Earth-saving initiative I was starting to pilot. A dark-haired, bespectacled man looked deeply interested in my potential program. After I was done talking, he came over, shook my hand, and introduced himself as Pastor Mike. "You know, you should really do this initiative at our church too," he said. "You should come and bring your family."

We went to church Sunday through Thursday, me holding Jeremy and having him take in all of God's lessons as a newborn. When we were back home from service, Harry noticed I looked upset.

"We're living in sin," I said, choked up. "We need to get married for this little baby."

Harry nodded. "I'd love that."

Unsure of who proposed to whom, we decided to become husband and wife for Jeremy. It was just further proof of how our beloved son changed our lives.

On our wedding day, Pastor Mike married us in our new church. I wore my sister Thelma's wedding dress. My mom and dad walked me down the aisle because it felt like my life was coming back together. Although my mom was not a perfect person, I still loved her, and since I didn't live with her anymore, it made life easier. Bernie was there, too. I grew the sunflowers and daisies for my bouquet in my backyard and tied them together with twine. The boys wore blue shorts and white dress shirts with little red ties and the girls wore floral dresses. There were no adults in the wedding, just our children. Harry's oldest son, Bryan, from his previous marriage, stood for him and Shaena stood for me. Jeremy was our ring-bearer.

For seven years, we had a beautiful life. Harry and I took the kids to soccer, went to church, worked together on our finances. People who didn't know us from before would've never known about Ocean City, or how he hurt me, or anything that had happened to us previously.

Harry and I were going to save the world. Still, it was never the same love after that. It was more of a mutually beneficial agreement where as long as Harry stayed sober, I was all in. He had to support my adventures and I was about to embark on a new one with Pastor Mike.

Chapter 11

Going to Otterbein United Methodist Church in Duncannon, Pennsylvania became more than a Sunday tradition for me. I also started taking Jeremy to choir practice on Tuesdays. His group was called Little Cherubs, he would jump up and down in his car seat, eager to let out his propulsive, hyper energy, trying their best to sing along with each other.

On this day, there was also something for me to get excited about: I had asked to meet with Pastor Mike about another project I wanted to work on in the church. He had supported my latest artistic venture: the Our World Project for my kids' school, where the class learned about the dangers of pollution and litter on a giant papier maché globe. The kids would pull off bits of litter and stick animals and fish all over the Earth.

As I walked inside the building with Jeremy, I saw other children running around, and one kid standing by himself with a dull look in his eyes. I looked to see if his parents were there, but he appeared to be all by himself. My heart sank, seeing a child like this. I kissed Jeremy on the forehead, opened the door to the choir room, and waved goodbye.

Then I walked down the hallway to Pastor Mike's office. I knocked on the light wooden door that was half-open. That's when he turned around and I saw him: a 5'7, semi-built, kind-eyed man with light brown hair and a light brown mustache and glasses. He was very sharp in his appearance, with a crisp collared shirt with a seam down the side of his sleeve and ironed slacks. He was sitting at a mahogany desk, writing left-handed on a piece of paper in front of him. Tidy piles of paper surrounded him. Different versions of the Bible rested in the bookshelves in the room, including the book *Who Moved My Cheese?*. We shook hands and I sat down in one of the plush guest chairs.

"Angel, the Our World Project is going so well," he said.

"That's why I wanted to meet with you," I said. "It's our job to advocate for these kids in school, and I want to do more for them outside of the church."

"These kids need to be more involved in art and sports," I said. "We can write a grant together to get this going."

"I'm in," said Pastor Mike. "And I have some ideas too."

I was excited. "Please, share them!"

Our one-hour meeting turned into two hours, with us brainstorming about how to raise money for our Children and Youth art program. Bake sales. Car washes. Sponsorships from individuals and businesspeople in the community. Suddenly, by the end of our time together, it felt doable instead of overwhelming. We were going to make a program for kids that they could afford and where they could flourish through camping, sports, and painting murals. It would be the childhood Mr. Stacks fought for me to have. I knew after looking at all I was creating, I must have felt how Mr. Stacks did: the one who gave all the hope to the kids. I was living as he did—as the voice of the kids. He could look down from heaven and know I was carrying on his legacy.

I began getting some of the mothers together to get the bake sales and car washes going. I had them fill out in-kind forms, meaning parents would trade their time for goods they needed. Some parents baked things, the kids helped with the car washes, other parents made schedules about manning the bake sales.

Then, I needed to create a non-profit, something that would provide for kids even when their parents couldn't provide for them. We made it our mission to assist children and families in need of tools to enhance their future. I wrote a community care grant that brought in $90,000 over the next three years. When I first saw this figure, I cried. Pastor Mike and I kept asking ourselves what we could create for these kids, and us succeeding in doing it. We funneled the money into a community resource center. The center was where we had the after-school program, the lending library, and everything the kids needed to succeed.

This, I knew as I was putting it together and finding donors, would become my legacy. I wanted to leave the program behind, and the mural would represent that. As the program blossomed, I began mentoring children who needed the most help. I swore I could almost feel the presence of Mr. Stacks with me as an eleventh grader apprenticed with me on a mural inside an elementary school. Bryson was a young boy, a football-playing kid with a thick build. He was one of the few Latino kids in a mostly white school, and I felt a special connection to him. The experience took me back to Scotland School and Milton Hershey, when I was once the odd person out. He was about to get placed into a juvenile detention center, but wanted to learn how to become a football player. We got him a job coaching the pee-wee teams.

As we painted, we realized we were both left-handed.

"We're the only people in our right minds," I joked. "We are really creative, us left-handers."

He laughed and agreed.

After our painting session, I dropped Bryson off at home. I had a bag of new paint tubes in my car. He gave me a big smile and a wave as I dropped him off and went back to school for my next class. When I parked, I began to look through my bag for the new tubes. They were gone. I furrowed my eyebrows. I'd just bought them this morning before seeing Bryson, and he had been sitting in the back of the car.

Could he have?

No, not Bryson.

Not like how I took Mr. Stacks' airbrush when I was his age.

I decided to see what would happen when I saw him tomorrow.

After teaching the class with replacement paints I bought along the way back to school, I found myself in Pastor Mike's office, sitting in a chair across from him again. I was feeling my confidence growing from doing this project, but I was also being reminded of my past. I'd been in so much trouble at such a young age, and there was hope for these kids to never experience the horrors of my own early life. Bryson seemed to be repeating my history, and I was there to watch. Perhaps if I could relate to Bryson like Mr. Stacks did with me, he'd be OK. Pastor Mike smiled warmly as I confided in him.

"You have an amazing gift," he said. "You don't have to be ashamed of what happened to you. Use this as a way to help people."

He was right. God had forgiven me and wouldn't ever hold me to the cross Jesus had already died on. Pastor Mike helped me stay strong in my faith that afternoon, and for the rest of my life.

About a week later, I came home from painting the mural, my arms, legs, and face dotted with shades of red, green, and blue. Taking a shower before starting dinner was high on my list, at least it was until I saw Harry sitting on the living room couch. I walked in and tried to give him a kiss "hello." But he moved his head. "C'mon, Harry," I said.

"I'm good, Angel," he said. "I just need a breath mint."

"Harry, seriously," I said. "What's going on here?"

He shrugged. "I'm just drinking at night to take the edge off the day," he said.

I fumed. I should have said more. I should have told him he was breaking his promise to me right in front of Jeremy, who was standing in the foyer. "Jeremy, why don't you go get cleaned up for dinner?" I said, hoping he would dart away. He didn't need to see his father this way, the way I never wanted him to experience or know at all. Jeremy ran into his room.

"You can't do this," I said to Harry. "We made promises to each other."

He shrugged. "I just had a hard day," he said, a little exasperated. "It's just this one time."

But the drinking didn't stop at evening bottles of Coors Light. Since he was an alcoholic, there was no way he was going to stop at one or two beers. I opened my newspaper to see how I was featured for receiving the Governor's Award for my work. The story was on the front page of the paper with an image of Governor Ridge, Shaena, and me. But as we read it, I gasped when I saw another photo on the second-to-last page in relation to a recent arrest. "Look, Mom, there's Dad," said Shaena with tears in her eyes. It was Harry's mugshot in the newspaper. I knew that he had been arrested, but I had no idea it would make the paper.

My eyes filled with tears and my heart raced. I became filled with dread. This was embarrassing. *What were all of these parents going to think after seeing this? Why couldn't we just have a great life with our children?* It was clear he wanted a different life than what I was creating. As tears formed, I realized I couldn't fix him anymore and that I could still love him, I just couldn't be with him.

I put my hand on Shaena's shoulder.

"I'm so sorry, sweetie," I said. She started to cry.

"All of my friends are going to see this," she said through tears.

"You can still make your own decisions," I said. "This doesn't affect your life."

Newspaper articles kept popping up for my program, Our Tomorrow's Future. *The Sentinel* interviewed me for an article in its "Your Neighbor" section, and featured a photo of me with big, curled, fluffy bangs and a gray flannel shirt. They wanted to show all the good work we were doing, and under a subheading in the article titled "Modest founder," I said, "God is the founder. I'm just the vessel for Him to work through." I felt that with all of my heart. Clearly, I wasn't ever going to stop the work I was doing. Harry wasn't going to stop what he was doing either. As I folded the newspaper and put it away, I made a resolution: it was finally time to move on and be emotionally and physically free from Harry.

Where I'd go was a completely separate question. I decided to go to Boulder, Colorado for an event presented by The Mind and Life Institute. Headquartered in Virginia, the Institute featured such visitors as the Dali Lama, and I knew Dr. Greenberg, who had given presentations based on the book *Destructive Emotions* by the Dali Lama. Dr. Greenberg and I were also working on a pilot program at Head Start. After applying for a grant for Our Tomorrow's Future and seeing Colorado's huge, snow-covered mountains, it seemed like a beautiful place to live. I managed to find a sales job in town that allowed me to earn a living.

With Harry about to go to prison again, I planned my escape. I took him back-and-forth to work release, and on the last day, I handed him the keys. "I've packed up the house and I'm leaving you," I said. He asked, "What's going on?"

"You promised me that Jeremy would never see you go to prison," I said. "But you broke that promise and we're not going to do this anymore." Then the tears formed. "You will do right for yourself and wherever you go and whoever you end up with, you cannot end up back in prison, it's not good for you. It's not a good example for the kids, either."

Harry got out of the car. He didn't try to convince me otherwise. I'd already packed up the house and the kids, and drove to Colorado. There was no looking back. Sal and EJ were relieved I was finally getting away from Harry, even though they would miss the kids.

On the drive over, I thought about all I had done so far, and about my last interaction with Bryson. I'd looked at him, knowing he'd taken those paints, and uttered the words Mr. Stacks had once said to me about his missing airbrush: someone else must have needed them more than I did. He shuffled his feet and sat in a chair in the art room we were in. I went into the attached kitchen area to make snacks for the class later on.

"Miss Angel, can I talk to you?" he asked. He'd left his bag on the table.

"What's up?" I asked.

Bryson was sitting with his legs stretched out and his arms over the back of a chair looking cool. "Miss Angel, I can't do this to you," he said. "I saw this stuff in your car and I wanted to take them home to paint, and when I saw them on the table, I just, well..." He trailed off. "I just didn't think. I just wanted them and took them without thinking it would hurt you. I'm really sorry."

He revealed the brush and several paint tubes he'd lifted from my studio from his bag. I put down my paring knife and came into the main art room. We stood looking at each other for a moment, and I could tell he was wondering how I was going to reprimand him. Little did he know, he was about to get the "Mr. Stacks" treatment.

"Bryson, you are so loved, and this decision you made to tell me this has changed your life," I said. "If you can remember to do this always, you will always do well."

Then I walked over to the supply cart.

"Pick out the brushes you want," I said. "Do you need a canvas?"

His expression of surprise turned into one of gratitude, or at least gratitude as expressed by an eleventh grader. "Thank you for teaching me. I'm worth it," he said.

These are beautiful beings, I thought. *If you focus on that, people will remember you for the rest of their lives.* What if Bryson could see he was a beautiful soul and could be forgiven just as Mr. Stacks had forgiven me for stealing the airbrush all those years ago?

As I reached the "Welcome to Colorado" road sign, I knew I'd made my mark on my old town. That day, I knew Bryson's life changed. And I was about to change mine.

I was new to Colorado and began working a sales job to not only make some extra money, but to better communicate with my art customers. I also started taking care of my personal life. I went to a life coaching event where I had visualized the man of my dreams. At this event, the organizers asked, "If you could pick the perfect spouse, who would it be?" I said, "He would be strong in his presence, that when he spoke, people would listen. He would be kind, but not self-centered." As I checked my Myspace account a few nights later, a handsome stranger living in Texas added me as a friend. I fell for this Puerto Rican man's chiseled, tanned face. I messaged him, and he said he was looking for friends.

"Would you like to be my friend?" he asked.

"Sure," I responded.

We talked back-and-forth for hours and hours, and shared our stories, both good and bad. Our childhoods had both been difficult, but we had worked to grow stronger through them. The more we talked, the more we fell in love. We told each other we would marry each other someday.

"I feel like we're already married," I joked. We set up a time to meet.

Jose and I met at a park and it was like we walked into heaven. It seemed as if we had met before, even if it wasn't in human form. By the time we got to the other end of the park, I was drunk on the color of his eyes and everything about him. When we parted, he smelled my hair, wanting to remember my scent. We kissed like I had never kissed before. I was drunk by the sight of him and the smell of him and the touch of his skin. I still am to this day.

"I'm in love with you," I said. I could feel he was in love with the unconditional love that I had for him. Our souls touched. It felt as if we had known each other all of our lives. This was my chance to live a new life on my own with someone I loved and treated me well.

Although my life was going in the right direction, I still had a superficial relationship with my mom. I had found my own voice working on Our Tomorrow's Future, and that God had forgiven me and I needed to be a good servant. My mom and I were two different people and that was acceptable. She was someone I would always love but would also sting my heart. I could forgive her as God had forgiven me and I could accept that, doing so was freeing for me. *But had I really closed my cycle with my mom?* I realized I healed myself already, but I was still surprised when I learned my true origin story from the DNA test.

Maybe it wasn't about forgiving my mom, because I'd already done that.

Maybe it was forgiving myself.

Maybe it's why I needed to see her.

I needed to see her in person to fully heal.

Chapter 12

Before I could return to Pennsylvania to see Mom, I had to prepare myself. I had to go deeper than I ever had emotionally, spiritually, or physically. To do this, I found a healer in Oakland, California through a friend from our Panama trip, someone we called by the nickname Ow. Her name was Nikki, and she was a community advocate. She and her significant other, TJ, ran the program that I wanted to delve into. TJ's head was shaved and seemed like a monk, while Nikki specialized in ayahuasca ceremonies. What could have been more beautiful than a monk and a shaman in love?

When Jose and I first arrived, the house was so warm and welcoming. Nikki and TJ ushered us into this great big space, which felt like summer camp because of the warm air and everyone hanging out together in one room, listening to our teachers. The couple was unique-looking: Ow had a red tinge to her hair, was down-to-earth, and easy-going. TJ shaved her head and wore an army jacket. They escorted us to the igloo outside with electricity. It was a dome-like building with rooms for each couple or individual who came to the retreat. Our room had little lights hung to the top of it that made it look as if fireflies dotted the ceiling, and there was an electric blanket on the bed to keep us warm during the chilly nights.

Before we walked into the ceremony room, TJ and Ow saged us in a big teepee to cleanse us of any negative energy. They used a bucket full of sage and palo santo sticks and flashed smoke all over us. Then, we took off our shoes and felt the cold green grass beneath our toes.

They also had a reading room where we would hang out and have morning conversations about our experiences. We'd sip unsalted vegetable broth for lunch among a wide range of books, which was our first food after fasting for eight to twelve hours, like we had in Panama. We were excited to eat the broth, hard-boiled eggs, carrots, and celery, although we still couldn't eat any meat and salts. It was key to understand discipline when it came to preparing our bodies for the ayahuasca ceremony to come since we would be confronted with very intense sensations.

When it was my turn to share with the group, my intent was to forgive my mom in a way that allowed me to love her completely, forgive her for when she reacted defensively to me and how this easily triggered me. To forgive myself and anyone I hurt in my past. It had been several months since my mother told me about where I came from. I was still very bitter and very shocked. I was still feeling very raw, dirty, knowing my biological father was a rapist. I was having panic attacks and feelings of unworthiness. Even so, I was hesitant to believe Mom's story. She had no concrete proof except for her side of what happened. The only person who would know the truth was long dead: my grandma, who Mom had called from Atlantic City. Without a paper trail, it was one of those times where I had to trust Mom's experiences. This seemed to be the first time Mom was authentic and vulnerable with me. The way she communicated felt like an awakening. *Wow, everything made sense. The breathing in the brown paper bag when she wasn't able to look at me. She was never able to look into my eyes in a loving way or tell me that she loved me. This is why she treated me the way she did.*

At this point, there was nothing else to trust. Still, in the sharing circle, I had a hard time articulating myself and being authentic. I felt like I was an imposter. As we sat together in this big room, we began preparing for the evening. I felt really uncomfortable with the group; as in Panama, I felt as if I didn't belong. Even though I was working through these feelings with my mom, I felt as if people would judge me. I flashed back to seeing Harry in the same newspaper I was featured in for my good work. Everything was coming at me and saying I wasn't worthy.

Jose started rubbing my hand and looking into my eyes. My shoulders relaxed. Unlike the time in the circle in Panama, his gaze and touch worked to calm me down. I began to feel my own worth within the group. This returned me to my intention: to forgive my mom. It was an intimate, connected time. I began to experience God's love, the universe, and the power greater than myself. I began to consider forgiving the most horrid of things that people do to each other, like those who hurt my mom. *We were all the children of this universe,* I realized. Forgiveness doesn't mean I had to endure abuse. And that was me. I could still make a difference.

The gong rang. It was time to prepare for the ayahuasca ceremony. At about 7:00 in the evening, Ow and TJ started preparing us with sage. We took off our shoes and sat in our designated spot, the same spot we'd first put our things. In the ayahuasca room, they played rhythmic drum music and we all sat and started with our intention. We took a pinch of tobacco from a bag, held it and made our intention before passing it to the next person.

There were rules to this ceremony. You had to ask for help from a shaman, not from your spouse or other people. Little glow-in-the-dark stars were on the floor to guide you to the restroom if you needed it. I watched each person approach the shaman as parishioners would a priest for communion. I kneeled down as Ow laid a blessing on the ayahuasca, and thanked her as I took the cup of muddy water. *Don't breathe out of your nose*, I kept telling myself. I was like a kid about to eat a worm. The mixture of two plants tasted like dead fish in my mouth. Putting ginger in my mouth beforehand helped only somewhat. Quietly, I went back to my designated spot, and Jose walked up right after me.

I laid down, closed my eyes, and waited for everyone to finish taking their ayahuasca. The lights began to dim, signaling that everyone was ready. They played Peruvian drums and shakers as the journey began. I allowed the substance to do its work, to face what I couldn't face on my own. It was like the movie *A Christmas Carol* going through the past, present, and future. I went through a trip seeing bad and good things all at once.

I began to witness and live through my mom's eyes. I saw all of her pain. I saw all of the reasons that I felt she did what she did. Why she treated me like she had. I couldn't imagine going through that. This had me feeling an abundance of love and forgiveness for her. How did she live with a child who was a product of one of the most traumatic moments of her life? I could see her not as this person who hurt me, but the person who was hurting. I felt so much more for her for the first time. I wanted her to feel the love I had for her, the same love that Mr. Stacks had helped me to feel for Shaena.

It all seemed to make sense.

Then I went on to see everyone this way: it was Harry, it was EJ.

Thoughts began shooting out of me. Emotions pummeled me like rocks.

EJ loved me but I couldn't love him back. I sought forgiveness from him.

I had to forgive myself for putting my children through abusive men.

I had to forgive myself and learn how to say "no" to Harry and Sal.

I kept holding onto what was familiar, but I had to let it go. We all had been hurting each other and I saw all of that in a rapid fire vision. The experience was like dying and going to heaven. I could replay my entire life. Every single hurt I'd made to another person whipped past me. I felt everything they must have felt. I had so much remorse, humility, and love. I sobbed and prayed. The experience was almost like a nightmare, and I asked Jesus for guidance and protection. I began throwing up and had to crawl over the glowing stars to the bathroom. I was throwing up all the junk inside of me, purging it from my body, physically and emotionally. The physical part, though, was all psychological. Some people with a lot of darkness inside purge a lot. I was purging, well, a middling amount.

I cried.

There was beauty in everything. Even me.

After this experience, I had so much hope. I felt a hundred pounds lighter. The chains I imprisoned myself with had been broken once and for all. The source within me had healed and forgiven me to a point where I could move forward. I could finally enjoy my life. As we got to Ow and TJ's gate to meet our Uber, I smelled the beautiful, crisp air as if it was the first time.

When I returned home, I knew it was time to reach out to my mom. I called and told her I'd visit. I wanted to witness her. Then I contacted a healer friend of mine named Tina who guided people through making peace with their repressed memories. I learned other ways to get through these things. I contacted her and she worked with me on some breathing techniques so I would continue to see my mother in her truth. I got on a plane. I was a little nervous, but I felt so much love in my heart for my mom.

It was cold and snowing outside, anticipating seeing my mom and sharing this love for her. She greeted me with some sense of apprehension. It might not have been everything I was feeling in my heart, but it was close enough. My mom was fiddling with her fingers. Her eyes filled with tears. As we talked and cried, all of those defenses between us seemed to melt away in that moment, at least that's how it felt for that moment.

As I was there with mom, I had so much love for her. I loved witnessing who she was. She was ready to get healed. I called Tina on Skype.

"Let your beauty show inside of you," said Tina. It felt different landing in Pennsylvania after many years. I had many people to see. Joann, my friend. Then my mom. It wasn't quite what I saw in my heart, but it was close enough. As I was driving through Harrisburg, I saw all of those streets that no longer brought me anxiety or fear. There was Dunkle Street, and I no longer felt angry about what happened to my bike and being left at school. I started to see freedom for all those chains that were keeping me defensive.

Mom looked at me, and I could feel she was genuinely sorry. I could see it in her eyes. For the first time, I felt like she was seeing me, and she felt sorry for how she had treated me. There were no walls, she was just there. I loved her more in this moment than I loved her ever in my life. I was sitting behind her while she was on the computer and I was energetically rocking her back-

and-forth and letting her know that she was loved. I was sorry for all of those things had happened to her, and I wished I could take it away.

"Can we just leave this on sound?" she asked, saying she didn't want the video on Skype.

"Mom, don't worry, you're beautiful," I said.

"I need to dye my hair!"

"No, I love your salt-and-pepper hair!"

As my mom breathed, she started talking about her childhood. Everything she said her mother did to her, she had done to me. Everything that happened to her had happened to me. I sent her love out with my hands. In my heart. I was rocking back-and-forth sitting behind her when Tina was talking to her like a baby, loving her as I always wanted her to love me. I forgave her. As she talked and cried, everything she said was how I felt. I felt her pain, because it was the same pain I experienced. I loved her more in that moment than I'd ever loved her in my life.

"I'm feeling pain in my stomach," said Mom.

"This is a part of the process," said Tina. "Continue to breathe."

I continued to be there for her as I had wanted her to be there for me. The truth is, I chose to come into this body to experience everything that was happening. I wasn't a victim of my world and I could choose the new path. I didn't need to be a victim of my mom's past. I could choose my own reality based on my free will. The sins of the father are passed on to the child until there is forgiveness. This was my awakening that I didn't need to punish myself anymore based on where I came from or how I was created. I finally knew who and what I was and how I served. I've learned in this moment that love is the only truth. We are all divinity in truth, expressing ourselves in whatever way we need to heal. We are here to receive healing or give it.

The little girl with the banana yellow bike was beyond a survivor. Now she could witness other people heal from their traumas. This girl carried her ability like a badge: the healing soul of a survivor. I believed once I got past being a victim, I didn't feel defensive anymore. I shifted out of that. I didn't need to be mad at Mom anymore either. She was divinity in form. She just had deep scars that had to be mended.

As I left my mother's house and looked up at the sky, I deeply felt we were all like the Golden Buddha. In Tibet, Golden Buddhas were covered in mud so no one could come and melt the gold down. Inside of us, we are like the gold, but we cover ourselves in mud. We coat our lives in things that don't make us feel golden, but that's what we are inside.

Sometimes we hide ourselves and our unworthiness because of what happened to us in our lives, no matter how old the hurts are. We're all forgiven and all we need to remember is to live a life in gratitude and instead of condemnation. While I backed out of Mom's driveway, I whispered the Ho'oponopono prayer, which I learned to say every time I saw someone hurting or remembered a hurt I endured: I am sorry. Please forgive me. Thank you. I love you.

Acknowledgements

A deep letter of gratitude to all of the mentors and teachers along my path: Mr. Clyde Stacks, Thelma Lehman, Bill Collier, Pastor Mike Brossman, Todd Tipton, Uncle Vinnie, Milton Hershey School, Tonya Scoggins, Mike Weller, and Joanne Aungst. Thank you for your loving ability to focus on the good in others when it could have been so easy to point out the flaws. These lessons have forever impacted my life, allowing me space to thrive, grow, and expand into more than I ever thought possible.

A very special thanks to Joanne Spataro for recording my story. You witnessed me raw and real without telling me I was right or wrong. You listened to my story without judgment and with a compassionate heart. The process of writing this book with you has been a profound healing experience with space to cry, mourn, and sit with whatever emotions I was feeling in any given moment. Thank you for your patience, for extending the deadline over and over for me to process and heal, for rewriting objectively without injecting any personal opinions or views. You will forever be dear to my heart as a brave warrior to endure it all as I relived it. Our time together was probably more effective than any counseling I've ever had!

To Wayne Scot Lukas. What a light of love! Thank you for the amazing cover design. Your love and passion for helping others heal is so humbling.

Mom, I pray we stay on this healing path together and can walk free in the light with our heads up without feeling judged or defensive. If not, I will do it in my heart. I love you always and unconditionally. I might be the perfect example of how something good can come from something horrible.

Dad, you will always be my dad. The truth of my origin will never change the love I have for you. Thank you for not letting it change the love you have for me.

To my grandparents, Mom and Dad: thank you for loving me the best you could.

To my beloved husband, Jose Ruiz. Thank you for your patience, kindness, and witnessing me with love and acceptance as we've grown on this healing path together. We have witnessed our defensiveness melt away into a river of love and appreciation. Thank you for loving me like you do.

Thank you to my children, Shaena, Billy, Jesse, and Jeremy. You're the reason I found healing and will continue to choose you again and again.

In loving memory of my daughter "Bee," left behind unnamed but not unwanted. I know you're with me. No words can change the ache in my heart for you. I'm sorry and I love you.